MW00356219

Leading Change
that Matters

Making Adoption a Reality

Published by KDi Asia Pte Ltd

www.kdiasia.com

Dr. Nancy Harkrider

Tan Kim Leng

ISBN:
978-981-07-8031-9

DEDICATION

With appreciation and in remembrance of Allan Friedman who personified the power of change and inspired all who knew him. His wise guidance and commitment in the early days of the company have been pivotal to our success.

And dedicated to individuals and organizations everywhere who make the world a more sustainable place when they adopt change that matters. Together we will continue to make a difference.

Table of Contents

Table of Figures

FOREWORD

If you were curious about this book, you are already interested in change. You know about organizations that have flattened hierarchies, streamlined procedures, or embraced mobile technologies in their quest to increase responsiveness and revenues. You know about the acceleration of the rate of change that foils expectations with waves of new unknowns. The US Army has a term for it: "Unk-Unks," which means Unknown Unknowns. But that doesn't tell you how to deal with it.

When my partner and I founded Ambient Insight in 2004, there was no such thing as Social Learning, or Location-based Learning, much less Mobile Learning value added service (VAS)—the digital learning landscape was much different five years ago, even two years ago. In my company's world of market analysis, change often means opportunity—an opportunity for a learning technology supplier to take advantage of shifts in cultural patterns, competition, and technology that predicts readiness of customers to buy new types of digital education products.

Navigating these changes is relatively simple compared to the challenge of creating a culture of change within an organization. We all know that "business as usual" will be out of business before long.

A journey through today's business environment is like whitewater rafting on a Class V river—it's fast, it's exciting, it's sometimes terrifying, even when you can see the rocks and drops coming up ahead. Even if you've paddled a river before, it's not the same river; unforeseen changes in the stream channel and water volume change the river. Class V is described as exceedingly difficult with long and violent rapids, obstructed riverbeds, and big drops—sounds a lot like today's business climate.

A leader's random exhortations to "paddle faster" aren't necessarily effective in whitewater conditions. While you never know what's around the next bend in the river, you can prepare paddlers to survive and thrive in the next set of rough rapids. To be successful, you as a business leader need to understand the nature of change (to the river, to a business, and to the people on board) and develop a shared framework of understanding how to quickly adapt and respond.

The old "command and control" approach went out back when computers came in. To be effective in today's world, change must combine a process-oriented and a people-centered approach that transforms stakeholders into committed participants of a deeper journey to understand, accept, embrace, and achieve sustainable change.

The sometimes satirical 19th century French novelist Alphonse Karr once said "plus ça change, plus c'est la même chose"—the more things change, the more things stay the same. His point was that turbulent changes don't affect reality on a deeper level. But the reality of business is that for serious change to take place it cannot be applied cosmetically—such as moving people and departments around like deck chairs—it must reach a deeper level and become part of the DNA of the organization.

That's what this book is about—a framework for moving beyond episodic change and towards navigating sustainable change.

Nancy and Kim Leng have taken the guesswork out of the unpredictable river; they have the expertise and experience for their roles as guides to a system for navigating unplanned change. The Change Facilitation Model and Adaptive Path Framework offered in this book can help you manage, implement, and evaluate change that matters.

Tyson Greer, CEO
Ambient Insight LLC

ACKNOWLEDGMENTS

Nancy would like to thank her children Sarah and Cody who continue to be wise beyond their years and incredibly supportive of a mother who often marches to a different drummer. And to her international circle of friends and colleagues who in every way encourage her to keep embracing change.

Kim Leng would like to thank his family for their support and love on a journey of self-discovery with international assignments that frequently require his absence from family. To his wife Lee Koon and son Denzel, he hopes his work on change inspires them as they have inspired his purpose in life.

To those who have supported us in the birthing of this book, longer than human gestation but thankfully not as long as that of an elephant, we want to acknowledge:

Our special thanks to Lim Swee Kim, who painstakingly improved the structure of the book and took care of all the formatting details both of us could have easily missed.

To Dr. Karen Devers who was instrumental in influencing the book's content architecture.

To Pat Reed, our copy editor, who promised a finished product that would be more readable without touching our narrative voice. She delivered on her promise.

To Cooper Williams, a talented designer, for polishing the graphics and making them shine.

To Douglas O'Loughlin, Dr. Patt Schwab, Joseph Teo and Dr. Charles Ling who reviewed early drafts.

And most particularly, to our KDi's colleagues, partners and clients whose stories make this book richly relevant as examples of adopting change that matters.

PREFACE

Reframing the meaning of change
is going to dramatically change the way you lead change

How this book is different   Are you frustrated with change models that over promise and under deliver? Are you ready to step into the winner's circle by leading change that really matters and is sustainable?

If so, ***Leading Change that Matters*** is for you. No more grandiose beginnings that flat line before they are ever implemented. No more wasted planning efforts. No more unrecoverable mistakes. Framed in case studies as powerful stories, this book will make you think, build your leadership skills, provide you with useful strategies and empower you to be a truly effective leader.

How our model prepares you to navigate chaotic, unplanned change
More and more, successful organizations are embracing the "long view" by using strategic, process-oriented, people-centered strategies. We have found that change is actualized with our clients when the power of our Adaptive Path is embedded in a high-stakes organizational challenge.

The Change Facilitation Model and Adaptive Path Framework featured in this book are based on two decades of client engagements in Asia, Africa, The Middle East and, most recently, in The Americas. As a planet, we are facing unfathomable changes and the pressing need to override our emotional hardwiring so we can get on with the critical business at hand.

A desire to share our knowledge with others
Sustainable change happens as you convert stakeholders from the uncommitted to active adopters. We know that's only possible if you win the minds and hearts of your people. That is the foundation of our philosophy and the purpose of ***Leading Change That Matters.***

We know when to step back and when to intervene so that your emerging skills support you in leading change that gets the right things accomplished. We look forward to learning about your organization's needs, your challenges and your vision.

DEFINING SUSTAINABLE CHANGE

In the context of change within organizations, here's our definition:

Change is something that dramatically shifts in our external world,
causing us to resist, then to consider, and ultimately
to adopt a more effective belief system.

While this definition appeals to the linear part of the brain, until the brain's emotional sector agrees, change, as we have defined it here, doesn't happen.

This tornado story by Nancy Harkrider shows how change vibrates with global relevance regardless of where in the world you call home:

> I grew up in a Texas farm family. In those days, farmhouses were built on brick pillars with crawl spaces underneath that were large enough for children to play in as well as to provide shelter for the dogs. These houses worked well for a lot of reasons but were dangerous in a tornado.
>
> My great-grandparents Tom and Mary Ann lived on the backside of my grandparents' farm in just such a farmhouse. One day, a tornado whipped the house off its foundation and took it skyward. Mary Ann, an unflappable farmwoman, happened to be standing at the kitchen sink when the tornado struck. As the house spun upward, she looked out the window and exclaimed: "My Lord, Tom, we're passing over William's peach orchard!"
>
> Their house landed in my grandmother's herb garden. When the rest of the family exited their storm cellar, afraid to think what had happened to their elders, they discovered Tom and Mary Ann sitting on the front porch of their transported house, none the worse for wear.

How did they survive? They stayed calm. They could see where the storm was taking them. After the tornado, they viewed their son's farm from an entirely different perspective. They appeared the same on the outside, but the experience left them forever changed. That's the kind of change we will explore in this book.

To this day, when anyone in my family experiences emotional upheaval, we describe it as "passing over William's peach orchard," and everyone understands that one of the relatives has experienced and consciously absorbed some kind of significant shift.

We strongly recommend you work with others to create a story that captures the hearts and minds of your people. Nothing resonates like a powerful story, one with a "stickiness" that goes beyond description. It truly gets to the heart of change.

INTRODUCTION

If leading change initiatives were easy, we would have it wrapped up by Wednesday afternoon, checked it off our task list, and left the office in time for an early dinner with friends.

This book is for leaders like you. It's based on our client engagements across multiple continents, where we have discovered what it takes not to simply manage a process but to effectively lead change. And let's be clear. Successful, sustainable change can only happen when you bring your internal and external stakeholders firmly onboard. When we say that's possible only if you win the hearts and minds of your people, we speak to the DNA of our philosophy and the purpose of this book.

Bottom line, it's all about people. We can guess that some of you are thinking that the systems, processes, and structures play a part in change effectiveness. We agree, but emphasize that people are designing those systems.

Organizational change needs to be led and facilitated so it deals with the complexity of human interactions. Leaving it to chance is almost certain to result in an unsuccessful or disastrous effort to implement change that is sustainable. Its success is dependent on Awareness, Acceptance, and Adoption by a majority of all stakeholders up and down the organizational chain.

You could line a wall of your office with books on change and innovation. Too many are based on sweeping generalities and a single-lens view from a helicopter. They always leave us feeling as though we have just been offered a sumptuous, gourmet meal only to discover when we arrive that the restaurant is closed. The reverse is the food court approach, offering wide options but nothing to guide us to food choices that will satisfy and sustain us.

Our Change Facilitation Model (see Figure 1) empowers a whole brain approach as the middle way. We help you ground your experience in understanding the how and why of people-centered change. Our method for planning change is not the usual linear project management approach. Instead, it is grounded in the inclusion of Change Support Networks as vibrant, mid-level conduits between impacted staff and senior management.

Then we design implementation strategies based on what we have found works for clients in diverse settings, with clear guidelines for why we chose these strategies, what is needed to make them effective, and how they can be evaluated.

Because it's not feasible to "front load" all the potentially new concepts in the Adaptive Path, don't expect yourself or others to be clear after your first reading on all the strategies and tools we recommend. We suggest you read first for understanding.

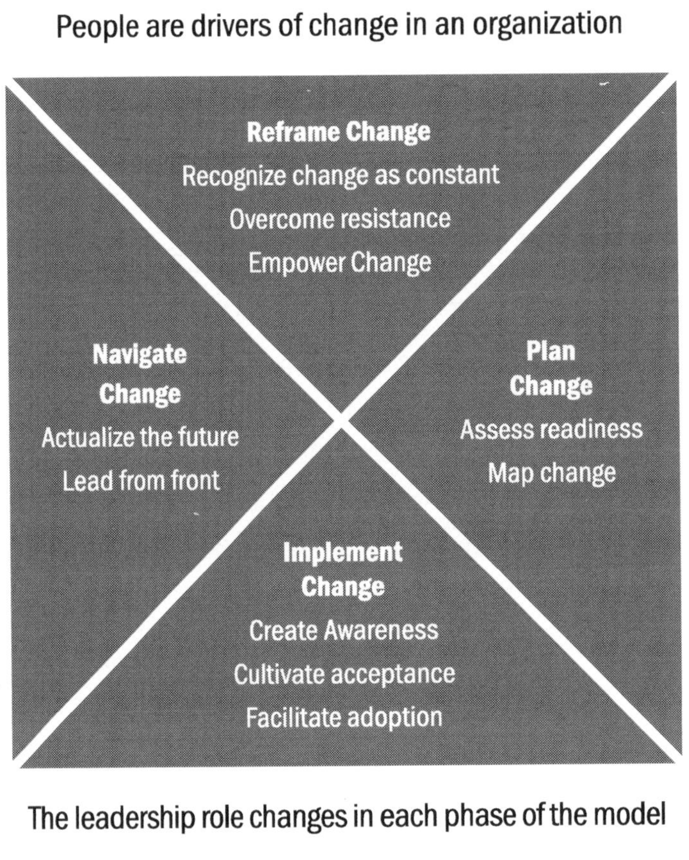

People are drivers of change in an organization

Reframe Change
Recognize change as constant
Overcome resistance
Empower Change

Navigate Change
Actualize the future
Lead from front

Plan Change
Assess readiness
Map change

Implement Change
Create Awareness
Cultivate acceptance
Facilitate adoption

The leadership role changes in each phase of the model

Figure 1 - KDi's Change Facilitation Model

**Reframe
Change**

Leadership Role

Explore change as a constant

Overcome resistance to change

Empower change

Reframing the Meaning of Change

What leaders need to know

Why Reframing the Meaning of Change is Essential

- The control mode for managing change isn't working anymore.

- The future, including ten minutes from now, is frightening and sometimes chaotic.

- Internalizing your role in this new world order means discovering resistance to change.

What It Takes for a Leader to Reframe Change

Take a deep breath!

- Find yourself an experienced coach. This is essential as you build skills in new ways of thinking so you can lead authentically.

- Be reassured that what you learn in this book will be invaluable in understanding this new style of leadership.

- Acknowledge that from day one of leading change, you are the model for how change can happen through a tested, middle-path model for sustainable change.

- Transparency and honesty about your own changes will build credibility with your team as you identify how to reframe change.

- You will need to remain strategic while being knowledgeable about all the elements of planning and implementation.

CHAPTER ONE
Exploring Change as a Constant

The great paradox of the 21ˢᵗ century is that, in this age of powerful technology, the biggest problems we face internationally are problems of the human soul.
– Ralph Peters, former U.S. Army lieutenant colonel

In This Chapter

Our choice of words for the title of Chapter One was intended to have you pause and consider the essential nature of change as a constant, both the planned as well as unplanned kind. It focuses on the strategic nature of leading sustainable change. Take advantage of the opportunity to think about the meaning of change for you and for your organization, to honestly explore your natural resistance to what you know is the necessary but sometimes uncomfortable reality of a dynamic that is here to stay. Gone is the certainty with which business worked in the twentieth century.

Your role and our mission

As a senior manager, you might have already been mandated to take an active role in your organization's mission to ride the waves of rapid change. If that isn't already on your agenda, it is certain to land on your desk in the near future. Or you might recognize that need in your organization and have a desire to make a strong case for a proactive change initiative. Our mission is to support you in broadening your perspective on the complexity of change by introducing you to useful, real-world strategies and tools to guide you through this process.

The telescopic view of management

We can safely assume that since you have opened this book, you are interested in discovering how you and your organization can anticipate and respond proactively to managing the uncontrollable, a contradiction in terms that we propose needs to become your mantra. Our intent with this high-level view is to illustrate the key need for Adoption as the only path to assuring viability and sustainability.

If the book is going to be helpful to you, it will be important for you to share with us the belief that change is constant and that, even though the future is uncontrollable, it can be managed proactively. With that in mind, let's begin our work together.

We can guarantee that, along the way, you will have varying levels of resistance. Chapter Two addresses this situation directly. We're suggesting you acknowledge that it's probably going to happen not only to others in your organization, but to you, sometimes when you least expect it. It is human nature for even highly committed leaders to discover their own pockets of resistance. In addition, as a professional and a more-than-competent manager, you have belief systems and experiences that make you legitimately question a change in business direction without compelling evidence that it is necessary. It is those very questions and the reflection about them that will make your organizational role more effective.

Here's the first in a series of simple techniques we have found valuable for our clients and ourselves. When you feel your defenses going up as you use this book, jot down your questions. *Why is this essential? How would I deal with this challenge? Why doesn't this make sense to me?* As you begin to work with the tools for planning and implementing change initiatives, you will leave what we refer to as "a question trail." Since change begins with questions, we believe such a list will be helpful in your challenge to manage the uncontrollable.

As we begin this journey together, you might want to consider asking yourself several key questions while you read and reflect.

- Does this make sense? What questions do I still have?
- How do these concepts help my organization?
- How do the concepts impact me personally?

Before we get to the "why" and the essential "how" of planning and implementation tools, we will share a high-level view of the elements of constant change so you get the telescope version before we zoom down to ground level.

Innovation and change in the twenty-first century

Media attention to innovation and change are popular news items these days. It's easy enough to assume you understand this concept, and we're certain you have a firm grasp or general understanding of many of the essentials. But all of us still have questions: *What do these changes mean to me? How is the twenty-first century different? Did someone suddenly flip a switch at midnight when 1999 became 2000?*

Even though it is tempting to believe the switch-on theory, it is, of course, too simplistic. While the global dynamics of the late twentieth century are propelling this new century, there are dramatic new shifts. The first order of business is to acknowledge the shift in cultural norms that were widely accept in the last century but are no longer viable in the twenty-first.

We have moved from a Resource Economy in the mid-to-late twentieth century to a Knowledge Economy in the twenty-first. The bridge between these two extremes was built in the 1990s, but it doesn't appear most organizations recognized and dealt with that shift. Those who crossed that bridge early and consciously have a definitive head start on the rest of the world.

In a social innovator's blog from the Ash Center for Democratic Governance and Innovation Initiative at the Harvard Kennedy School of Government, Sarah Horowitz and Maya Enista have identified three trends that offer a window into considering how twenty-first century organizations are different.

- Digital tools are cost efficient and reach many more people, promoting transparent and inclusive dialogue as well as allowing for authentic, user-created content.

- Leaders who organize across cultural and geographic boundaries and are moving away from the hierarchical norms of the mid-twentieth century are the drivers of these changing demographics.

- Our social compact is in flux. The problem-solving capacity of business and government is increasingly dwarfed in comparison to today's social needs. More groups are mobilizing their own constituencies to provide collective benefits and resources and to advocate for change on behalf of their members.

Innovation needs highly impacted stakeholders onboard

Every change initiative plays out as an emphasis on a particular cluster of stakeholders. For example, if you need to create a new communication system for your external partners and it has little or no impact on your employees, that's a relatively simple change project. If it involves shifting mind-sets and skills training for the sales force to deal with a new communication system, the complexity can increase dramatically.

It is dangerous to assume when making changes that primarily affect one of your stakeholder groups that none of your other stakeholder groups will be impacted. Consider how many touch points a sales team and its senior managers have on other parts of the organization. If the sales team digs in its heels, its complaints have an impact across the organization. And it is no surprise that what will quickly follow is a drop in sales productivity. At that point, every stakeholder from the bottom to the top of your organization, every external partner, every stockholder, the media, and the industries that are your largest customers can all get involved in a downward spiral. Remember that card game where you carefully set the cards on end in an elaborate spiral? Touching the first one could flatten the entire deck.

Our perspective on organizational change

Over several decades, KDi has become a thought leader, first in Singapore, then across Asia and now in Africa and the Middle East. With all our clients, we emphasize that change in organizations from a Resource Economy in the mid-to-late twentieth century to the current Knowledge Economy is dramatic. It is critical for forward-thinking organizations to acknowledge that, more than tacit agreement, the necessity for proactive change is absolutely essential.

The four dimensions, as depicted in Figure 2 , show the ways in which much of the world has moved from a Resource Economy to a Knowledge Economy. They are the ones we believe are foundational for sustainable change:

- **From product to performance**
  While the world must have products as fuel for the economy, the more essential, sustainable issue today is focused on the "how" for increasing stakeholder adoption that results in increased performance.

- **From functionality to processes and capabilities**
  This orientation is a necessary shift so organizations can fulfill the needs of their stakeholders.

- **From task-based to project-based opportunities**
  This shift will propel organizations to a leadership position because they value diverse opinions and collaborative involvement.

- **From sourcing internally to including partnership networks**
  These networks take advantage of both talented people within the organization as well as strategic external partners.

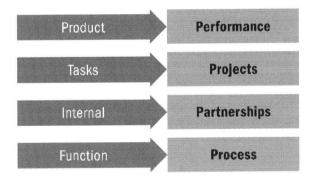

Figure 2 - Four Dimensions of Sustainable Change

All of these dimensions speak to the bridge from the twentieth century to the twenty-first and the importance of using what you learned in the Resource Economy to respond to the new challenges of both the present and the future of the Knowledge Economy. Just as importantly, it is essential that you "unlearn" what worked twenty years ago, or even a month ago, to make room for proactive responses to change.

We applaud the work of Karl Weick and Kathleen Sutcliffe, two thought leaders who wrote *Managing the Unexpected*. Their fundamental message, based on their research with what they refer to as "high reliability organizations," speaks to mindfulness and anticipation. They include:

- Tracking small failures
- Resisting oversimplification
- Remaining sensitive to operations
- Maintaining capabilities for resilience
- Taking advantage of shifting locations of expertise

Another person whose work we admire is John Kotter, a professor emeritus at the Harvard Business School, whose area of expertise is leadership and change. He emphatically bridges the migration from the twentieth century to the twenty-first through his work with challenges found in change initiatives. His classic work, Leading Change, is as viable today as when it was written in 1996.

Using the broad-stroke work of people like Kotter, our consultancy applies these high-level theories to our model for addressing change through a process that becomes operational on the ground rather than at the helicopter level.

More and more, sustainably successful organizations are internally organized around strategic, structural, process-oriented, and people-centered activities.

Acknowledging and working with challenges

In their book, *Management Reset: Organizing for Sustainable Effectiveness*, Ed Lawyer and Chris Worley have identified four core challenges that take a broadly sustainable view of the way organizations should be managed. Regardless of an organization's political culture or mission, the efficacy of these core values should resonate for all of us.

- **The way value is created**
  Lawyer and Worley emphasize that robust strategies are preferable to strictly competitive ones. While it is true that unless an organization is competitive, it will cease to exist, it is also true that if it doesn't base that competition on the agility of innovative thinking, it is taking the shortsighted view.

- **The way work is organized**
Sustainable organizations "need a design that makes them adaptable, responsive to changing conditions, and responsive to multiple stakeholders. The structure, work processes, and management process need to facilitate innovation and execution, collaboration and efficiency."

- **The way people are treated**
This foundational concept focuses on nurturing talent based on employees' competencies. The key to success for organizations that create value through such competencies mirrors what we now understand about attracting, retaining, developing, and motivating talent.

- **The way behavior is guided**
"How employees behave is strongly influenced by the combination of their organization's leadership style and culture. Sustainable management organizations need to be led with an approach that creates leaders throughout the organization and that rejects the imperial chief executive officer model. They need a culture that loves change, innovation, and sustainable performance."

Qualities of the resilient manager

Kim Leng tells a story about a conversation with a senior manager in Tanzania who queried him with this question:

> *I can see how evolving countries like ours have so much catch up work to do that we will always be in the business of change. But why is that true of advanced countries like Singapore?*

Kim Leng understood where this manager's question was coming from, especially since the challenges are indeed significant in places like Africa. His answer, however, surprised this senior manager. Kim Leng pointed out that every country, no matter where it is on the development arc, faces unexpected events of minor and major magnitude that require resilient leadership as an essential ingredient for success.

That reality levels the playing field.

We have identified a number of essential qualities for the resilient manager. Note that we did not use superlatives like "exemplary" or "superior." An individual who has psychological resilience demonstrates a clear ability to cope with stress and adversity. He or she is able to recoil or spring back into shape after bending, stretching, or being compressed.

Becoming a change agent means being involved and thriving over the long haul. The twenty-first century's assault on much of what you have taken as givens means you can never consider a change initiative completed. It simply goes through evolutionary migrations.

If that disturbs you, consider this old adage: if you aren't part of the solution, you're part of the problem. Our take on that old adage is this: you can stand still and get run over or you can lead the pack and trail blaze for others. The race, however, is not a one-time win, but a series of relays in which you pass the baton to others.

The qualities we believe are most important speak to who we are as well as what we are becoming. They include:

- **Eagerness to learn**
  The world is full of discoveries for a lifetime of learning and knowledge pursuit.

- **Courage to try**
  Without exploring new paths, no new discoveries and experience would be possible. The only real failure is succumbing to fear.

- **Shrewdness to inspire**
  Through others, we extend ourselves and help people move toward greatness by overcoming obstacles. While shrewdness traditionally could mean manipulation, we believe the positive side of this trait is about using our persuasive skills to coach and inspire others.

- **Desire to influence**
  If you are a manager, others along the way saw and rewarded your ability to influence and control. Keep in mind, however, that, under stress, the desire to control can keep you from being flexible about changing mindsets.

- **Resilience in dealing with peaks and valleys**
  Resilience is tested most dramatically when you sit in the front seat of that roller coaster called change. So as you climb onboard, be ready for a sometimes frightening, frequently exhilarating, life-changing ride.

Key attributes of empowering change

Here are the attributes we have identified based on our work with governments and organizations in emerging countries.

- Managing change facilitates project implementation, an integral part of any project initiative.

- Committing to alignment creates a common understanding of business objectives and strategy for change initiatives.

- Focusing on communication gets all expectations and concerns from key stakeholders pinned down early.

- Modeling a culture of encouragement builds trust, support, and commitment to implementing change.

- Acknowledging people's resistance is effective when you listen consciously to their fears and address their concerns effectively. People often get onboard early and easily once their differences of opinion have been listened to and honored.

- Exploiting early success by involving people directly, whatever their job description, is an early indicator of success. Their enthusiasm spreads to others.

Where do we go from here?

We believe that paying attention to benefits is key for effectively leading initiatives and will pay sustainable dividends.

Before we drill down to practical strategies for leading change initiatives, it's essential that we explore the underlying reasons why change at warp speed is a complex challenge for every organization and why people resist change.

So we'll say here what you will find repeated regularly in this book. It's about people, first, last, and always. No grand mega-events, no rubberstamp CEO messages, no carefully crafted mission and position papers will be effective unless you find ways to change the hearts and minds of your stakeholders, the people who are most heavily impacted by change.

If senior managers know they need to change some beliefs to be successful leaders in a world of rapid change, why do we all, in one-way or another, resist change?

As we move to Chapter Two, some of the answers might surprise you.

CHAPTER TWO
Overcoming Resistance to Change

The fates lead those who will. Those who won't, they drag.
— Old Roman saying

In This Chapter

Rather than glossing over the need for change as a given, we have elected to signal, with its own chapter, the importance of changing the way we change.

We define change in the context of a sustainable middle path, exploring why we resist internal change in order to thrive on the potential for change, and then we consider the shifts required to move past limiting mind-sets.

There is change and then there is change. The change we are talking about is the change that lets us manage the unexpected and innovate in ways that allow us to successfully ride the waves of those uncontrollable events. As we noted in Chapter One, the need for a proactive approach to all manner of change is the one given we have in an increasingly uncertain world.

It's absolutely true that change initiatives for change's sake are not useful. All of us have experienced these well meaning but misguided attempts as paths to nowhere.

We strongly encourage you to read this chapter carefully and refer to it as you and your team move through the Change Facilitation Model for sustainable change. The key term to keep in mind is sustainable.

Why we resist what we know is good for us

The simple answer is because we are human. We have been resisting change in the emotional part of our brain since birth.

It starts when we are young. We are sad to leave our kindergarten class, and someplace still in our unconscious is the parental voice that says enthusiastically, "change to real school will be good for you." When we reach puberty, we again get that change mantra. And then there is the unrequited first love. By the time we reach adulthood, we've had a great many change-is-good-for-you life events that definitely didn't feel good at the time and have left lingering debris in our unconscious.

And what happened each time? We resisted change, and almost certainly we felt the emotional sting of events over which we had no control. Paul MacLean, a neuroscientist, has reminded us that the greatest language barrier "lies between man and his animal brain (where) the neural machinery does not exist for intercommunication in verbal terms."

That means our current belief systems reside mostly in our nonverbal limbic brain where beliefs aren't accessible in the same way as our frontal lobe handles our conscious thinking. So while our mature, logical self agrees that embracing change in order to effectively manage that process is an imperative, our emotional brain wants to walk or perhaps run away. And while we might physically remain in the room and think we are eagerly ready for change, our emotional brain has checked out. This means we now need to make a conscious effort to honor the emotional brain and its role in our being human, but not allow it to control our authentic leadership abilities.

As Kim Leng describes it, "We have difficulty in accepting data or facts that fall outside our mental model of the world. Until we commit to and practice revising and expanding our mental model, we are trapped seeing the world in only one way."

Managerial myths left over from the old economy

MYTH: **You should only react to change you can see.**

REALITY: If you were a fortuneteller, you might be able to "see" problems before they surface and identify global hiccups in advance of the event. Any organizational culture that models riding the waves of change is psychologically prepared regardless of what the future throws at it.

MYTH: **If it's not broken, don't fix it.**

REALITY: The world might have functioned that way during the Industrial Revolution, but in the Knowledge Economy, you can't observe things that are broken until it's too late.

Perhaps you subscribe to the we-have-no-problems-here mentality. Maybe you are experiencing damaging undercurrents of staff dissatisfaction or an unanticipated surge in new competition. Ultimately, you could find yourself in the middle of the ocean, going down for the third time, when you suddenly have that moment of clarity.

MYTH: **Implementing many changes is good because you are bound to get one of them right.**

REALITY: This plays out as the ready-fire-aim strategy. As we will continue to emphasize, there are no multiple chances to get it right because your stakeholders will quickly label you as a person who doesn't know what you are doing or, even worse, isn't transparent. This is deadly in getting your stakeholders to believe in new change initiatives.

MYTH: **It is possible to plan and execute change projects without any amendments.**

REALITY: This is the check-it-off-the-list-and-it's-done mentality. If there is evidence that your planning or implementation is ineffective, be transparent and do it quickly. Apologies, when they are delivered as management's response to concerns and a desire to be more effective, will have all but the hardcore naysayers willing to give the project implementation another chance.

MYTH: **The pace of change happens as a single event.**

REALITY: Nothing could be further from the truth. Unless you are thrown into emergency mode, which happens with, say, a traumatic weather event that shuts everything down, change happens as a constant cycle of innovation that grows and evolves.

Ways we humans exhibit resistance

We have identified five distinct sources that cause resistance to changing mind-sets, all originating in our "emotional" brain. When we offer our theory about resistance to clients, it almost always initiates some surprise, then interesting discussions resulting in reflective thinking, and sometimes some "pushback".

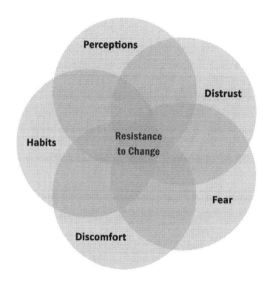

Figure 3 - Key Reasons for Resistance to Change

We listen carefully to our clients, honoring their resistance while offering strategies for moving past ineffective mind-sets. If you have that same respectful attitude toward your stakeholders, they are likely to have a more positive response to change.

Here's our list:

- **Fear is a de-motivator for change**
  The fear factor pins us in place, and we even have physical symptoms associated with it. Not surprisingly, fear resides in our emotional/limbic region at the base of our skull. Is it any wonder that it's common to see people rub the back of their neck when they are under stress?
  Fear can be called many things, including "the unknown," "failure," "leaving your comfort zone," or "loss of face."

- **Trust and distrust are two sides of the same coin**
  A deeply primal emotion is our early-warning radar that flags whether or not we can trust a situation. This is a healthy safeguard against new, untested situations.

  While fear is based on automatic reactions that have little or nothing to do with current reality, our trust/no-trust radar is often based on situations that have actually happened in our work lives. The protective part of our brains signal us to either shut down or adopt a wait-and-see attitude. Unless we have been unbelievably lucky, we have experienced some trust issues in our business lives, making it easier to understand the resistance you and your team can encounter as you begin the implementation stage where stakeholders have enormous impact.

- **Discomfort with unfamiliar ideas**
  Humankind has adapted and thrived through deep patterning of survival skills. Those subspecies of humans that didn't learn to override old skills and adapt to updated ones make interesting archaeological finds, but nothing else. Psychologists have labeled our discomfort as "cognitive dissonance," a condition that finds us on the bridge between our comfortable mind-sets and the need we can see on the other side for a more effective way of operating in a world defined by dramatic change.

- **Perceptions hold you back but also allow you to go forward**
  Selective perception, hard-wired in that unconscious region of our brain, becomes personal filtering and results in our unique view of the world. However, with conscious awareness, you can use your existing menu of perceptions as interpretations to help you select how to perceive and act on new or modified stimuli.

- **Habits both protect you and trap you**
  You are a walking bundle of habits, far too numerous to list. Again you are looking at a double-edged sword. Habits allow you to be efficient; to filter out what needs to be done rather than to do everything that could possibly be done.

  You also have deeply entrenched habits you wish didn't belong to you. Whether it's something as simple, say, as drumming your fingers on the table when you are thinking or yelling when you are angry, these habits are hard-wired, requiring a conscious effort to change, or at least, to manage effectively. And just in case this fails to resonate with you, in the morning, try something relatively simple like brushing your teeth with the other hand.

Our goal here and throughout the book is not to provide definitive written-in-stone recommendations. You will have your own lists of issues, and it's valuable to name them, consider them, and then make a reasoned decision about how to handle these issues in the present and future.

One thing is certain. Belief systems, rooted in the emotional sector of our brain, result in fear and trust issues. And they pretty much cover the territorial view of resistance. Understanding the origins of people's resistance helps you first sort out your own issues and then empowers empathy that others recognize and learn to trust.

Innovation is anything but business as usual.
– Anonymous

Paradigm shifts are essential to embracing change

Think of a paradigm shift as a change from one way of thinking to another. It's a revolution as well as a transformation. It doesn't happen to an organization spontaneously, but is driven by those who see themselves as change facilitators.

Remember that every morning when you look in the mirror, you are seeing someone who owns the accountability of leadership and wants to constantly improve. This is the opposite of the myth that change is instantaneous across an organization. The paradigm shifts in thinking for you and your team need to be ongoing. The sustainable version of that shift is continuous wherever you are in a particular change-initiative cycle.

All we ask at this point is that you commit to planning, implementation, and evaluation based on legitimately bringing your stakeholders onboard.

It begins by acknowledging that your change initiatives are doomed to failure without them. Your knowledge will evolve in a variety of ways from this point.

This book isn't primarily about theory, but this is one instance where we believe a short theoretical summary can deepen your understanding of the term "paradigm shifts."

In 1962, Thomas Kuhn, a physicist and philosopher of science, wrote *The Structure of Scientific Revolution* in which he fathered, defined, and popularized the concept of "paradigm shift." Kuhn argues in his book that scientific advancement is not evolutionary but is a "series of peaceful interludes punctuated by intellectually violent revolutions," and in those revolutions, "one conceptual world view is replaced by another." It is interesting to note that Kuhn, one of the early connectors to the twenty-first century, was far ahead of his time. Kuhn notes "awareness is prerequisite to all acceptable changes of theory."

We all have the capacity to change

The difference is what we do with that capability. It begins in the mind of each individual. What we perceive, whether conscious or unconscious, is subject to the limitations and distortions produced by our inherited and socially conditioned nature. However, this does not restrict us because humans are clearly capable of change. As it turns out, this resistance to change was actually a good thing for our ancestors. But we are facing unfathomable change and the need to override our emotional hardwiring so we can get on with the critical business at hand.

First and foremost, we need to acknowledge the influence of our emotional brain as our protector when we sense danger. That empowers us to become adept at separating new realities from ineffective, outdated belief systems. That's when leading by example takes on real leadership dimensions.

It's impossible to be an authentic leader without the self-realization that we share the basic nature of our humanness with those who look to us for leadership. The difference is that we are all discovering ways on our own to make that paradigm leap. If you are lucky, you have colleagues or friends who are willing to dialogue about change from a strategically sustainable perspective. And if not, a search for a few of those types of people should be at the top of your to-do list.

Now that the groundwork is in place, it's time to assume your leadership role in managing for the uncontrollable. Our consultancy is an early adapter of this change paradigm. Our expertise and the lessons we have learned have global reach with clients and key relationships in Asia, Africa, the Middle East, and North America.

In 2004, our consultancy convened a diverse group of speakers for a full-day seminar in Singapore. Titled "The Adaptive Edge: Enabling Organizational Transformation and Innovation," the event evidenced our organization's position as agents of change. Principals in our firm spoke on global perspectives, a systems approach to enabling change, and lessons learned from the speed of change.

Case studies from the private banking sector and a government agency provided compelling late twentieth century evidence that paradigm shifts are possible. "Embracing Change: The ICA Journey" revealed the action behind these success stories.

The case study offered by the Immigration and Checkpoints Authority – a government agency usually called the ICA – demonstrated how several groups involved with Singapore's border control security managed to merge successfully. In what had the potential for a dynamic of fear and mistrust, a carefully designed and skillfully orchestrated plan was put into action.

The Director of Planning and Technology for the new authority described the complexities of this merger, noting that paradigm shifts were never easy. Because the leadership was able to draw people into its shared vision, it actualized a robust mental model so people could accept the new authority with trust and support. The speaker closed his presentation by noting that "perhaps it's too soon to make conclusions, but we think we are beginning to feel like a family." Today Singapore's ICA has withstood the test of time and is a strong testament as a model for that illusive but essential paradigm shift.

Mosquitoes as models for successful adaptation

Mosquitoes – astonishingly – can teach us something. Nancy turned up the volume on her car radio when she heard the first words of this story:

Imagine how tough life would be if raindrops weighed three tons apiece as they plunged out of the sky at warp speed. That is how raindrops look to a mosquito, yet a raindrop weighing fifty times more than a mosquito can hit that mosquito, and the tiny insect will survive unscathed.

How is this possible? Here's how researcher David Hu, an assistant professor of mechanical engineering at the Georgia Institute of Technology in the United States, describes his research:

"Put yourself in a mosquito's shoes, or rain boots, for a moment and step outside into a downpour of seemingly gigantic raindrops. They're basically plummeting comets falling all around you. You'd think a mosquito wouldn't stand a chance. We expected a similar thing to happen as driving your car through bugs and you see them splattering on your car windows."

Yet mosquitoes clearly survive close encounters with raindrops. So Hu's group set out to run an experiment that made the most of their skills as mechanical engineers and biologists. "Hitting a mosquito with a raindrop is a difficult experiment," Hu confirmed. "The first thing we did was drop small drops of rain from the third floor of our building onto a container of mosquitoes, and you can imagine that didn't go very well. It's kind of like playing the worst game of darts you can imagine."

Undaunted, the team took the experiment inside. They fired jets of water drops at the mosquitoes and recorded the results with a super-high-speed video camera. They found that mosquitoes don't actually dodge raindrops – they hitch a ride. You read correctly. According to Hu, "as the raindrop falls, rather than resisting the raindrop, they basically join together kind of like a stowaway on this comet." So as a result, they meet very little force. To them it's like getting hit with a feather. They ride the drop for about a thousandth of a second until their wings catch the wind like little kites, and pull the mosquito away from the drop. The mosquitoes don't seem any the worse for wear."

And here's the lesson for all of us

"The real hazard for mosquitoes is apparently when they are flying very close to the ground. If they don't peel off from the raindrop in time, they live out that axiom about being between a rock and a hard place." In human terms, Hu reminds us, you would basically get smashed if you were standing on the ground when a piano fell on you.

The obvious extension of this logic is this: if we prefer to thrive on change rather than being flattened by it, we need to pay attention to strategies learned from the lowly mosquito.

Where do we go from here?

We hope by now you are beginning to acknowledge that people are at the heart of any successful change initiative. If that still doesn't sit comfortably with your belief system about what it takes to be a successful leader, we strongly recommend you suspend your skepticism while we introduce you to specific strategies for how you can exhibit new leadership skills for leading from the front.

As you have seen, taking personal responsibility for our intention to thrive rather than being trapped in old mindsets is a personal responsibility. Your evolving skills come into play as you lead your team using motivational strategies that allow your organization to "hitch a ride" instead of getting pummeled by rapid change.

This is the point in our journey when we begin the process of building our knowledge about the key principles of leading sustainable change. We accomplish this by understanding what gets in the way of change for all of us, and then committing to the personal paradigms all of us need to adopt.

CHAPTER THREE
Empowering Change

Efforts and courage are not enough without purpose and direction.
— John F. Kennedy, U.S. President

In This Chapter

We now begin the process of understanding the key principles and framework for facilitating change. And that leads us to the need to identify and involve stakeholders by building a broad, deep coalition of support for empowering change.

We encourage you to remain open to our proposal. Reflection and discussion before you and your team spring into action is absolutely essential for success. Otherwise you might intellectually accept the shift to people-centric change, only to revert back to business as usual.

Surveying the landscape before beginning the journey

Isn't it curious that we never plan a holiday without considering the possibilities based on needs and desire for the destination we ultimately select, including what we might want to do there, who we likely want to see, and even the restaurants we would like to experience?

And yet we all charge off on our horses to conquer the uncertain future, immediately dropping our helmet visors so we see nothing except a narrow slice of a broad landscape. Something is seriously wrong with this picture. As Kim Leng succinctly expresses it, "This critical first step needs to be framed so it is less about planning and more about setting up all the critical ingredients to make this whole thing work."

Be forewarned. This new way of beginning a project will be uncomfortable at best. Incubation doesn't come easily for classically trained managers. Unless tasks are being ticked off, meetings held, and reports submitted on time, we tend to believe and deeply feel that nothing is happening.

Throughout the rest of this book, we will provide you with thinking and doing strategies as you and your team internalize the concept that projects are successful because the right groups of people are identified and onboard. They fail when that key element is ignored. Keeping people at the center of your change initiatives is the only path for increasing your chances of success.

You are going to frequently encounter the key term "stakeholder". Here's what it means in the context of this book and our people-focused framework: stakeholders are diverse internal and external populations that are impacted in some way by the proposed change initiative. Some of these stakeholders might become a key element in influencing the planning and implementation of the initiative. For example, if the government requires a school system to change its requirements for graduation, school principals will be directly impacted in multiple ways and are key stakeholders in this change initiative. They can also be instrumental as a part of the core team, providing invaluable insider knowledge.

This is where our Change Support Network comes into play, a concept we will introduce in detail in the next chapter. It will be an essential element as you navigate continuous change.

Rest assured, we will get to the more systematic elements of effectively managing a project, but first let's focus on a people-centric framework. We are firm about what it takes to make organizations and the initiatives they undertake successful. The bottom line is this: stakeholders are essential to success. We all need them. And we need access to more of our own brain's bandwidth to lead, coach, cajole, and encourage people impacted by change to give us their best effort.

A doable, scalable planning perspective

Planning has gotten a bad reputation, partially because in the tradition-based world, once the planning document is nailed down, there is no looking back or looking any direction for that matter. This is the opposite of our belief. We think the path to change initiatives is an adaptive one, requiring a broad view paired with a drill-down to specifics.

Consider the plans that are collecting dust after you, your team, and your organization all put so much effort into them. As the saying goes, "been there; done that."

And then there are the failed change projects that might well have been doomed before the managing director made the announcement of "an initiative that changes the way our organization does business." If every organization could achieve that total ownership espoused by the majority of change-management consultants, the world would tilt on its axis, and we would have everything in place to make that paradigm shift to a Knowledge Economy. None of us need hold our breath waiting for that to happen.

We believe change initiatives are about proactively anticipating the future in order to manage the unexpected. It is about selecting projects with high need, acknowledged by the majority of stakeholders as possible and scalable. It is also, at its core, about people, and in case anyone has missed this, people are unpredictable.

Most of our lives are lived on autopilot,
not only because of our assumptions about how life works
but because of our assumptions about ourselves.

Art Markman, a University of Texas professor whose research explores thinking, reminds us of the importance of understanding we are wired genetically to be unpredictable. Using this information about others and ourselves makes us better communicators. It also holds the key to understanding our role in change initiatives. Markman believes "our world is a constant tradeoff between exploiting choices that have been good to us in the past and exploring new options. If we only exploit, then we run the risk that we will not notice change in the world that makes the option we are choosing worse than it was or makes other options in the world better than they had been when we first explored the world."

Time to push the reset button

Twyla Tharp, the renowned choreographer, observed: "before you can think outside the box, you have to start with the box."

What's the first thing you think of when you are asked to lead a new project? Do you focus on the procedurals of scheduling meetings, finding a location for the work sessions, and establishing agendas? We guarantee if you stick with this linear response to the challenge of reacting proactively to future events, your project is doomed to failure.

Granted we need to start with the structure of that box, but it's a different box than the ones we have created in the past. Imagine a box shaped like a hexagon. It looks solid but can be rotated in different directions, each giving us a different perspective on the challenge. And if we tap into a perspective that interests us, it opens, allowing us to explore new ideas from a different angle.

The first order of business is to reframe, then refocus our "internal landscape." If you haven't already read Spencer Johnson's *Who Moved My Cheese?* , we recommend you do so as soon as possible. If you read it when it was first published, revisit it, and seriously consider buying copies for your team. In the book, the character Haw realizes, "it was natural for change to continually occur, whether you expect it to or not. Change could surprise you only if you didn't expect it and weren't looking for it." This reframing/refocusing begins by broadening your view and allowing for multiple perspectives, not simply making decisions routinely from your personal telescope.

Our commitment is to empower you with useful, real-world strategies and tools to guide you through this process so you participate in and respond proactively to "managing the uncontrollable." We can only be surprised if we don't anticipate the change and if we don't have a frame of reference for dealing with it.

Adaptive thinking as a way of reframing

There's a distinction between adaptive thinking and the term "innovation" as it is generally used. Nancy describes an interview she found really impactful. With Steven Johnson, the author of the book *Where Good Ideas Come From*. Nancy was intrigued by what Johnson calls "the adjacent possible," a term he used to indicate situations in which ideas work because they are connected to something else.

She was struck by how much this concept aptly described the framework we use in client collaborations. More about this later, but we suggest you mentally file away the theory of "the adjacent possible" and use it to recognize and consider places in your organization where this concept can link experience with adaptive thinking. This will enable your projects to address a specific shift in your organization.

In Chapter Two, we noted the double-edged sword — why you achieved your position and how it has now created challenges from the new demands on your professional future. Someone has moved your cheese, but you can use your traditional skills, linked to the need to reframe, to figure out that it's no longer about finding the next location for another cheese supply. It's about building your skills to figure out what you can't yet actualize by taking those first steps down an adaptive-thinking path. At this point in this chapter, as in all the succeeding chapters, we will provide you with specific recommendations you can use as "thinking" and "doing" tools.

And here is a non-negotiable, fundamental cornerstone for your success as a team: unless you can get a majority, or at least a "tipping point" of management and staff buy-ins as well as that of external stakeholders, the game is over. Agreed, that was meant to catch your attention, but the statement stands.

> **Reframing the meaning of change**
> is going to dramatically change the way you lead change.

Our Adaptive Path Framework

Our framework for change as shown in Figure 4 was developed over time as a realistic, sustainable process required for stakeholders to get onboard. It is based on these principles:

- Change adoption is an adaptive process, not an event.
- Team leaders have responsibility for outcomes.
- People must be the focus if change is to be facilitated.
- How change is perceived will strongly influence its outcome.
- Ownership at all levels is key to sustaining the change.
- Embracing a call to action has to work at the individual level.

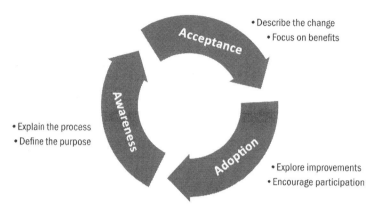

Encourage and Navigate Change

Figure 4 - Stages in the Adaptive Path Framework

This framework didn't get sketched quickly on a notepad at a company management meeting. Here is how Kim Lang describes our framework:

> This was a reflective process over time with our client engagements. We observed the frustration of client attempts to be innovative and manage for the unexpected while, at the same time, operating from the old models of the last century. This created disconnects that were insurmountable. What was missing was a pathway for making that migration from the Resource Economy to the Knowledge Economy.

Each of the three stages of our framework must be planned and implemented consciously and rigorously. That's why we devote time to describing and offering tools for each element of the framework in the planning and implementation stages.

Awareness is based on a logical approach that uses the conscious brain. People need to understand what the initiative is about and why it is important. Stakeholders need to understand the future is based on this change. If they resist, their position should still be treated with respect. As you will discover shortly, that doesn't mean they are written off as terminally negative. It means that winning hearts and minds begins with respect.

Your team can take this valuable feedback from the Awareness campaign and integrate it into the Acceptance stage, which must emanate from the heart and the emotional brain. For all stakeholders, this involves emotional buy-in. This is particularly true with staff members who are understandably focused on their own needs since they don't have the power to make changes in the organization. They need to know how it will affect and benefit them.

> Here's a classic example of the difference in Awareness and Acceptance. Ask people if they know that exercise is essential to good health, and all hands go up. That's Awareness, and the logical brain knows this to be true. Now ask how many exercise regularly, and only a small percentage of hands go up. This is the point where the heart and emotional brain kick in and where an initiative either loses ground or gains enough momentum to reach that all-important tipping point.

Only then will people be ready to move on to Adoption, where their involvement is action-oriented. Without a commitment and follow through in the Acceptance and Adoption stages, change is not sustainable.

Consider this all-too-common scenario

Top management decides their company needs to shift its location in order to have larger facilities and be closer to major customers. So far, so good since these are proactive decisions to ensure sustainable outcomes. But the scenario often goes sideways from here.

It never occurs to management that the people most affected are staff members, and the patterns of their lives revolve around the proximity of home to work and the complications in transport if those patterns change. The CEO delivers the news through a video broadcast posted on the company website, and supervisors are asked to break the news to their employees. The rumor mill starts churning right away. Staff productivity falls immediately. People are angry and stressed. And management from its telescope perspective probably doesn't have a clue that they have a disaster on their hands.

In this scenario, the all-important Awareness and Acceptance stages are too often forgotten entirely or executed poorly. Equally deadly to the success of any change initiative is to confuse the purpose of the Awareness and Acceptance stages. We have found that it is absolutely essential to consider and execute each stage as separate components. It's no wonder the Adoption cycle, and the cultivation required to make it happen, all too often don't bear fruit.

We developed an effective strategy for drawing staff into this process when we worked with a Singapore Government Ministry that needed to gain support for the adoption of a new employee intranet. Instead of using a more traditional way of drawing employees' attention to the change, we worked with the ministry's internal team in creating an innovative approach that included the best aspects of experiential learning. Here's how it worked.

> The ministry announced a contest would be held and five posters created. Each poster was placed in one of five different sections in the ministry's headquarters. The posters were created so employees had to find all five of them, decipher a hidden element of the message and put it together.
>
> The contest was challenging and fun, giving people the choice to work as a team or as individuals. It is an excellent example of injecting a fresh idea, such as branding, to push Awareness. The tagline for the new intranet was "knowledge shared is knowledge gained," a relevant, highly effective jump-start for the Awareness stage of the Adaptive Path.

Looking at the same landscape but seeing it differently

Every senior manager is aware, and sometimes painfully so, that communication and trust between senior and middle management and middle management and staff leaves much to be desired.

The figure 5 on the next page, illustrates the differences in the way you see change and how others in the organization view that same change.

We recommend you begin to think both metaphorically and practically about differences in upper management, middle management, and staff so you can play to those differences as strengths rather than weaknesses.

Acknowledge that the goal of the Change Facilitation Team is to gather intelligence, make sense of new learning, and facilitate the change based on a cycle of Awareness, Acceptance and Adoption.

Figure 5 - Organizational Perspectives

Upper Management:
Organizational leaders view the world through a telescope. This means those in upper management see their jobs strategically. They ponder such questions as these: *How does this impact the organization? How does this affect my ability to be a successful high-quality leader by looking into the future and guiding others into that future?*

Middle Management:
The macroscopic view offers communication flexibility. Don't be concerned if "macroscopic" is a new term for you, but if you were a physics major, you probably know it.

It means large enough to be visible to the naked eye and focuses on comprehensive analysis of large units. That's because middle management needs to operate up and down the chain of command.

Middle management includes staff supervisors, and it has the important job of translating what's going on with staff to senior management. Middle managers worry about effectiveness and control. *"How does this affect my team's performance and my ability to exercise control?"* Middle managers don't have the executive long view but need to be able to understand it. In every respect, their jobs might be more complicated and require more diverse skills than either senior management or staff. They bring invaluable perspective to the planning and implementation process.

Staff Members:

A microscopic view is based on needs and limitations. Not surprisingly, staff can be found headed straight for the microscopic view when change is imminent. They see change through the microscope's close-up lens, asking the single but potent question, *"How does this impact me?"* Their response is emotionally based because all they manage is their own lives. Their power to influence change is based on initial and sometimes long-term resistance. Your challenge is to bring staff members onboard, constantly reminding yourself they are essential for sustainability in any change initiative.

Remember the discussion in Chapter Two about resistance to change? As managers, most of our thinking to date has been logically based, housed in the middle of our frontal lobe. This might be the reason we slap our foreheads when something becomes clear. What is challenging for managers is getting access to their limbic, emotional brain.

And it follows that staff functions from a microscopic view is squarely centered in the emotional brain. Not surprisingly, they are challenged in the need to think logically and reflectively. Their relationship to their job generally ends when they walk out the door to go home. Conversely, managers often have trouble turning off their "office brain" and the lingering stress of their work challenges.

Essential to honor world views different than our own

As you move from the challenge of dealing with your own restricted view of the world, you will also be responsible for communicating effectively with staff members who have a different model of the world than you do. All the challenges of communication about change are based on this simple-but-perplexing puzzle. The key to communication is based on being aware of, honoring, and working with these differences to get your staff onboard. This challenge for effectively modeling leadership and transparency requires you to achieve a balance between the linear skills you already have and the new skills you need to build in order to effectively lead change initiatives.

> ***Things we fear most in organizations*** *– fluctuations, disturbances, imbalances – are the primary sources of creativity.*
> – Margaret J. Wheatley, organizational behavior consultant

Here's an example of that difference in the telescopic, macroscopic, and microscopic views. Let's return to the story about upper management making a strategic decision to move the company's headquarters to an area near their largest customers. Senior and middle managers can easily kick into high gear. There is so much that needs to be done to make certain the move has been planned well and executed flawlessly. Can you feel the manage-and-control strengths taking over your logical brain by simply considering the daunting task list your role requires you to execute?

Meanwhile, in their cubicles, on the production floor and in the company cafeteria, rumors abound. All the microscope-centric employees had an emotional reaction to your well-crafted, all-company announcement, and it definitively wasn't the enthusiastic acceptance you had assumed – or at least had hoped for. If you sat still and listened from your office, you could hear the rumblings and feel the vibrations in other parts of the building.

Why would that be? Clearly, that physical move might cause many staff members inconvenience or worse in their daily lives. They will have to figure out different modes of transportation and different routines for hectic morning and evening schedules. And for parents who wear many hats or staff members who are trying to better themselves by taking night courses, that inconvenience can become a major headache.

Why didn't anyone ask them their opinion? They might be asking themselves if management even cares that this move will increase their stress levels. The discontent gets more vocal as the planned move approaches. Many other staffers have likely joined those who were most vocal after the initial announcement.

We are not suggesting that management's decision to shift locations was wrong, but we are suggesting it is essential to consider and involve staff in decisions that directly impact them.

People at the heart of the change landscape

A firm grasp of the people landscape has to be in place before formal planning begins. We will continue to remind you that the key to your success is understanding all the stakeholder groups and appreciating what they will contribute to, or detract from, your initiatives. This is about a people environment, supported by the business processes at which you already excel.

Stakeholders are groups you need to communicate with and keep informed. Some of those stakeholders should become part of the inner planning circle. If we don't embrace the stakeholders in both these roles, we don't have an accurate view of the landscape.

As a part of this process, you and your team will be conducting a Stakeholder Analysis, and we will be providing background and tools for this process. The core team needs support so they become part of the tipping point within the support network. This is a critical element in implementing a robust Change Facilitation Team that will lead change initiatives. These points will be covered in Chapter Five.

This process takes more time up front but empowers that critical telescopic view only achievable when you have representatives of different perspectives who can translate their views. Note that this plan will have a different mental model if you are leading a team in your own company than if you are a consultant working with a client.

It would be easy to assume that if you are in charge of a change initiative in your own organization, you automatically have a pulse on every level of the organization. But it is impossible to have all three views at once. It would be more straightforward if you were working in a landscape with no humans and you were able to plan with the serenity of knowing that everything would fall into place as you had envisioned it.

The reality is that you are dealing with the unpredictable nature and chaos of people and their subcultures, and you clearly have your work cut out for you. Be assured it is a role you can consciously and successfully grow into.

What you need to become an empowered leader

As you prepare for the next two chapters on planning, here are some considerations to keep in mind for leading your team:

- **Plan for diversity on your team.**
  If everyone is a clone who has your style, you will certainly be comfortable working together: in fact, you will be too comfortable. Innovation comes from a positive, emotionally safe environment that honors differences and embraces new ideas.

- **Bring new blood to the team.**
  Such people are the future of the company and can make unique contributions. Welcome them, encouraging your more senior people to become mentors.

- **Acknowledge upfront challenges** and work with your team on strategies that avoid – or at least mitigate – team burnout.

  We encourage our clients to release key team leaders from part or all of their present job responsibilities. When key team members are overburdened, they fall into negative mind-sets rather than the model of inspired, effective leaders and change agents who navigate a strong Adaptive Path.

- **Remind yourself and your team that change is always a process**, never an event. If it is a singular event, no matter how traumatic, it can be worked through because the challenges are immediate and obvious.

- **It's now about balance.**
  You got where you are by your strong ability to manage and control. Those skills are still valuable, but you are going to need to hone others that you will have to practice to reframe what you do with that structure called planning and implementation.

- **Find ways to get more comfortable with ambiguity.**
  You will need to learn to be more comfortable with uncertainty. Like Haw, the character that lost his cheese supply, you will want to feel some excitement, or at least some twitches, about this new way of managing the unexpected. The power of the uncertain future is not only about the goals

of the project but the process for getting there. Both are valuable in building your own resilience and modeling it for your team as well as the wide range of stakeholders who will need to get onboard.

- **You will be required to sell the concept**
  Identify a team member who has the most natural affinity with the people in the executive offices and other members who have respect and regular interface with staff. These messengers' inclusive, transparent approach will be the same up or down the chain, but their communication will be sensitive to differences in worldviews. In our framework, these messengers, who make up the Change Support Network, are a dynamic and essential element to success.

- **Nothing drains a team's energy like inefficiency**
  As you and your team strategically plan for meeting project objectives, consider the "how" of process. For example, if you need to get some input from two of your team leaders about an essential procedure, you wouldn't schedule a face-to-face meeting. Instead, if you use conference or Skype calls, you save time and energy for everyone.

Where do we go from here?

This is a good place to pause and ask some questions.

- Is change for its own sake good?
- Are we in danger of evangelizing organizational change as uniformly desirable?
- What criteria can guide us in reflecting and then acting on these critical questions?

At this point in the Adaptive Path process, you and your team have reflected on and participated in essential dialogues to identify the necessities of following an adaptive philosophy. Now, dealing with resistance mitigated by effective communication, you will be prepared to move intuitively but assertively to the more structured phase of assessing readiness.

Keep in your conscious mind this challenge for senior managers.

You were hired to manage and control, and now you have to deal with the tools of change where you will encounter the full range of human unpredictably as well as overt and covert resistance.

This is hard work, but it's the kind of hard work that is also energizing and rewarding. It is possible for individuals, groups, and, yes, even organizations, to discover that responding to change offers personal rewards and helps people become stronger, more proactive, flexible contributors.

Now that you have surveyed the landscape and have some awareness, and, we hope, acceptance of a new way of managing, you are ready to assess your readiness for planning the change initiative.

If you have been impatient with what you have read in this chapter, we suggest you leave it for a while and then read it again. Staying open to the benefits for how the Adaptive Path increases your potential for becoming an exceptional change agent-empowered leader.

Reflecting on the Meaning of Change

An Exercise to Accept Different Points of View

Using the telescope/macroscope/microscope metaphor (page 35), give your team opportunity to consider the challenges they face in dealing with different viewpoints than their own.

It will be helpful if you use the graphic as a handout or a large poster since everyone thinks more dynamically and creatively if they see an image before they use a lot of words.

Ask what the graphic means to them and then suggest they complete these statements:

"For senior management, this project is like _____ "
"For middle management, this project is like _____ "
"For staff, this project is like _____ "

Completing these statements can lead to valuable discussion, including the realization that it is much easier to finish the sentence for your own job title and more difficult to conceptualize it for someone else.

Then guide the discussion to what this implies about the differences in effective communication for various job functions up and down the organization.

Recommendation: Making use of these types of exercises throughout the project cycle will minimize communication disconnects before they happen.

Leadership Role

Assess the readiness for change
Map the change

**Plan
Change**

Why Planning Adaptive Change Is Essential

- Planning for adaptive change requires changing some mind-sets to "reframe the meaning of change" during planning.

- A well-conceived and executed needs assessment is crucial. Then "map" it to find the connections that will make adaptive planning possible.

- Without that conscious intent, guided by meaningful criteria, planning will be done the way it always has, leaving implementation to limp to the finish line.

What It Takes for a Leader to Plan for Adaptive Change

- Be a learner, along with your team. Your team will be encouraged to discover that you are a learner yourself on this Adaptive Path.

- Remind yourself and others that the traditional project management mind-set is more than a professionally learned skill. People with natural project management skills have been managing events and people even before they could talk.

- Honor what makes you and your team good at what you do because it's not a matter of throwing out the old to embrace the new. It always has to do with conscious intent.

- Become adept at really listening to your Change Support Network as they bring you messages about the concerns of highly impacted stakeholders.

- Remain strategic while building your knowledge of developing a people-centric plan for change.

CHAPTER FOUR
Assessing Change Readiness

*It doesn't matter that you get where you thought you wanted to go
if it's not where you need to be when you get there.*
— Author Unknown

In This Chapter

Embracing the concept of assessing change readiness will alter the way you think about and support transformational leadership. Why, you might ask, should we make assessing readiness for change a separate set of activities from planning for change? Over two decades ago, our consultancy began to consider how to add viability to facilitating change.

Assessing Readiness is critical to the Adaptive Path planning process. Skipping this step brings new meaning to the term "putting the cart before the horse." While planning is focused on valid project management practices, this chapter is primarily about people. It's also about team leadership in collaboration with the Change Support Network.

In this chapter, you will discover the power of the messengers who provide insider information about highly impacted stakeholders. You will learn why assessment is not an overnight task but is also not a protracted process. It is concise, targeted, and based on needs analysis. By the time you freeze your findings and move on to the action plan described in Chapter Five, you will be prepared to use what you have learned to create a Change Adoption Plan that converts your stakeholders to enthusiastic adopters.

Evaluating readiness authentically

We have found in client consultations that many organizations have a long-established pattern: they skip assessing readiness or give it only a light touch before moving on to a more traditional planning process.

We feel so strongly about this phase as a distinct process that, based on our consultations in diverse settings, we are putting our credibility on the line with this next statement. The rest of the initiative will suffer if the needs analysis process is not taken seriously and executed effectively. We'll coach you on how to identify and lead from the front. The next planning chapter offers you food for thought and some practical tools.

Key Terms for Assessing Readiness

Details, examples, exercises, and client experiences will be explored in future chapters. At this point, a broad understanding of key terms is sufficient for us to move forward.

- **Stakeholders are people affected by the change.**
  They are usually groups of people who are a part of large community based on their profession, social grouping, or business relationships. Depending on the type of change initiative, junior staff members might make up a major stakeholder group if they are most impacted. Another initiative might have minor impact on employees but a major impact on external groups such as channel partners.

- **The Change Facilitation Team considers viable strategies.**
  They then design and test market a Change Adoption Plan in preparation for initiating the critical Change Communication Plan with the goal of achieving broad-based support from all key stakeholders.

- **Change Support Networks are unique.**
  They represent both the general categories of stakeholders and provide key information from multiple frames of reference. Their involvement in the project gives them a unique perspective that enable them to become supporters of the current initiative within their own spheres of influence. You might never have encountered the concept of a Change Support Network. We believe it is of critical importance for reality checks and expanded awareness in order to minimize the danger that the Change Facilitation Team will make decisions based on its own frame of reference rather than that of impacted stakeholders.

  To differentiate, the Change Support Network is a small group carefully selected from the stakeholders that collaborate with the Change

Facilitation Team in analyzing change readiness. It has a long-term, more diversified relationship with the Change Facilitation Team through its middle-manager networks and grounded in a type of personality that relates well up and down your organization.

- **The Change Adoption Plan is approached strategically.**
  A detailed plan that is the foundation for getting a change initiative under way, it is the basis for effective planning and implementing with groups most affected by change. It is crafted to address the ways people react to change and help them to embrace it systematically.

And a note of caution before we continue

It is human nature to fall into the trap of labeling certain people or groups within your organization as "permanently resistant" to any change, large or small. This places the responsibility where it belongs, on you, as leaders, and, in collaboration with the Change Support Network, to identify the specific aspect of the change that is causing resistance, making it easier to identify ways to address and mitigate stakeholder concerns.

Approach for Assessing Readiness

Assessment is achieved through distinctly critical steps. At its core is the Change Facilitation Team. Starting from that core, you will consider your own resistance to change, rate your readiness for change, and select those who will assist you with that process. Then the circle moves to the Change Support Network who will be providing you with invaluable insider information. As the sponsor for the Change Facilitation Team, you and your team leader will be bringing the Change Support Network onboard by introducing its members to the Adaptive Path Framework of Awareness, Acceptance and Adoption.

Moving from assessment to drafting the Change Adoption Plan and then into the implementation phase, the concentric layers within the circle widen and deepen. There is tangible benefit to return again to the concept of the spectrum from resistance to readiness for change and how that is manifesting itself at a particular phase of the project.

And because people are often unpredictable, a group of employees or customers who initially supported your change mandate might fall off the

Adoption wagon if there are hiccups or major adjustments. This is, of course, the nature of managing the unexpected. You won't simply be managing external events over which you have no control but, in addition, those events you need to anticipate. You will be dealing in one way or another with unexpected responses and likely some resistance from your internal and external stakeholders.

If you and your team have been aware of the volatility of people's responses over time and if you have learned from that process, you will be ahead of the game with the implementation stages of this initiative. You also will find it useful when planning begins for the next wave of change. The essence of passing along knowledge that matters happens when team members reflect on what they are learning as they lead.

> **Consider This:** Say to yourself every day:
> I expect the unexpected and prepare every day for the next wave.

This is not an overnight process

At this point in the change facilitation process, you and your team have reflected on and participated in essential dialogues to identify the essentials of following a change management philosophy.

Did something about this last statement bother you? We have now reached the point at which most change management books start making assumptions about paradigm shifts with you and your team. It sometimes appears there is an assumption you woke up this morning, looked in the mirror, and saw a telescopic vision of your change initiative in which everything, including support from all quarters, fell into place.

We don't believe this is how shifts in perception and behavior happen. What is more natural, and definitely more likely, is that you and at least some of your team might continue to have some resistance and questions about this new way of managing change. We believe the Adaptive Path, while assessing readiness for change, respects resistance in all of us by dealing with questions both consciously and strategically. It is only in "the doing" that a shift in perspective evolves. That shift comes with action and becomes a part of our core when we reflect with others and ourselves on what happens when we are in action mode.

Note we didn't mention arrival at that perfect state, since that isn't possible. Staying conscious of shifts in how we think, however, results in new insights for how to lead with integrity. And for the record, questions, supported by the evolving belief that other good questions lead to new awareness, get you where you want to go. So ask questions, encourage them from others, and applaud those who ask them.

Now that we have surveyed the landscape and you are open to a new way of thinking about change, we will begin the discussion of the role of readiness as an essential addition to the traditional planning process.

Still feeling some resistance? All the more reason to plunge into this chapter where the tools you use with your team in assessing stakeholder readiness will also be your personal guide. And it is essential to make sure the leader and the learner inside each of us is talking to each other.

Managing leadership concerns

Before we move on to the key action elements of this chapter, we'd like to introduce you to a concept with important implications at every stage of the Adaptive Path, whether it's your first time managing a key initiative or your twentieth.

The process of understanding your own motivations and value system must begin with the Change Facilitation Team. As your team addresses its own concerns, it needs to begin to consider how it will manage that process with all key stakeholder groups, internal as well as external.

Once the team begins to internalize the value of assessment, its members need to turn their attention to how that will play out over the life cycle of the project, keeping both the philosophy and strategic implementation for communicating with stakeholders in balance with project implementation tasks and timetables.

Teams we work with have found it helpful to consider three broad types of concerns: operational, assumptive, and emotive. Identifying the source of a concern leads to strategies for listening to, honoring, and then mitigating those concerns. We began this chapter with high-level bullet points. The rest of this chapter deals with the details of how and when you effectively plan for and assess readiness before moving to project implementation.

Keep these three categories of concerns in mind as elemental for the work you do together and the bridging skills you will need to work with the Change Support Network as well as the project team. If we only deal strategically, we leave concerns and opportunities on the table. Small things, strategically set in the larger concepts, make all the difference in sustainable change. We get our arms around large things by understanding the small things.

The chart below illustrates examples of specific tasks representing components of each major element of a change project. To make certain you are staying on track, it's essential to routinely shift from the panoramic view to the detail view and back again. This is key to validating decisions.

Type	Example	Characteristics	Approaches
Operational Concerns	Changing cash payments to electronic payments will require all customers to have access to electronic means Some customers might not be able to adopt this change if they cannot afford the technology	Presented as barriers or obstacles that will take more time and resources to handle. If these concerns are not addressed, they will create work-related problems in Adoption of the system	Find working solutions. Need to handle head-on in the Change Adoption Plan
Emotive Concerns	New management directive requires all managers to give up individual workspace and share a smaller clustered workspace due to cost-cutting measure	Comes across as personal feeling of distress and loss Happens to everyone if the loss is perceived to be great	Lost prestige, entitlement, or pace of change is too fast. Need to listen and empathize

Type	Example	Characteristics	Approaches
Assumptive Concerns	Employees might be unhappy with the new attendance system because they have concerns that the system will track their movement and invade their privacy.	Doubts or presumptions that might lead to unmanageable situations Generated due to lack of facts or relevant information	Need to investigate further and clarify with relevant stakeholders Reclassify as operational or emotive concerns

Our experience tells us your team cannot deal effectively with the complexity of these concerns in isolation. You will be partnering with the Change Support Network to gauge the readiness of the organization by reviewing the nature of concerns that the support network brings to the table.

From the beginning, we recommend the team consistently ask:

- Which category of concern is this?
- How does that point to the type of information you need to understand the underlying meaning behind the concern?
- What does that meaning tell you about communication strategies you need to implement?

Stakeholder pushback should increase your commitment to the importance of finding legitimate ways to bring as many of the non-committed as possible onboard.

> **Consider This**: Remember that every concern is legitimate to the individual or group with that concern.

Keys to the kingdom

The strategy for your using members of your Change Support Network as messengers is the missing link not found in most other models. These carefully selected middle managers and supervisors can effectively interpret concerns up and down the chain because they represent or are members of one of the highly impacted stakeholder groups.

They are like runners in ancient civilizations, carrying messages from one kingdom to another so that leaders in both kingdoms received and sent information. But unlike kings who sometimes had the messenger executed, you are going to listen to, engage, and collaborate with your Change Support Network. You might want to read this paragraph again since we have just offered you the "keys to the kingdom."

The flipside of this equation is this: waiting for all stakeholders to fully embrace change is neither reasonable nor viable.

What you will need are people who are willing to set out on the Adaptive Path because your team has done its homework in assessing readiness using the following steps:

- Test the water to determine the readiness level of key stakeholder groups.

- Be aware that the more concerns, especially the operational and emotive ones, the more resistance stakeholder groups are likely to exhibit.

- Confirm that assumptive concerns are clarified and reviewed along with operational and emotive ones.

Only then can you assess whether the project is ready to move to implementation. At this point, we advise adjusting the pace of the Adaptive Path implementation to ensure issues are addressed, based on their importance to the organization.

Identifying a strong candidate for team lead

Your leading candidates will be managers who are able to keep project goals in mind while paying attention to communication strategies that are responsive to stakeholders. In our work with developed as well as developing countries, we have always been able to collaborate with our clients in finding an experienced manager with good people skills.

The ideal Change Facilitation Lead should have these skill sets in order to:

- Enhance competencies to meet the needs of the project activities
- Model and coach to enhance transition competencies
- Facilitate planning the transition
- Assess readiness of the stakeholders through needs analysis
- Define suitable communication strategies to generate awareness

And that's just the planning stage. The Change Facilitation Lead also needs to:

- Serve as an active member of the Implementation Team
- Provide insight and recommendations for communicating and listening to stakeholders and then model a strong commitment to implementation
- Promote learning and development for adopting new practices

Over the cycle of the project, the lead will:

- Facilitate change adoption planning
- Conduct Stakeholder Analysis and Readiness Assessment
- Define effective communications solutions to stakeholders
- Collaborate systematically with the Change Support Network
- Promote learning and development for adopting new practices

At this point, if you have already been assigned this role, you might want to take a few deep breaths or possibly blow into a paper bag until you are no longer dizzy. (This is our attempt at a little humor.) You will definitely not be alone in the process since you will be bringing quality people onboard with specific skills to take on key elements of the transition.

Questions for team lead candidates to ask themselves

- Do I have the ability to meet the defined expectations?
- Which skills do I have that will be critical and useful?
- Which skills or knowledge do I need to sharpen?
- How do I recover when something doesn't work out as planned?
- What can I do to improve current realities?

- Will I be able to cope with the pressure?
- Will my sponsor arrange for others to take part of my workload while I am involved in this role?

Criteria for selecting a Change Facilitation Team

As the Change Facilitation Lead, and before you begin jotting down names that come to mind for the team, remember that to be successful, you need to consider function first and then find people with skills in that function. Since your mandate is on the people side of the equation, you need to look for skill diversity and a commonality or at least an interest, if not direct experience, in working with stakeholder groups.

The readiness assessment will be an important benchmark for every phase of transition planning and implementation.

As you begin to work on a list of possible team members, and using the consideration guidelines we provide here, rate each possible member for what you believe to be their capacity and readiness for change. If you don't have personal experience with people on your short list, ask their colleagues how they would rate a prospect. This is your first opportunity in selecting your own team to begin using people-focused criteria for selecting the Change Facilitation Team.

The Change Facilitation Team has a distinctive, multifaceted role. It oversees the startup stage, works with the Change Support Network to weigh stakeholder concerns, analyzes those findings, and plays a key role with the project team in implementing the Change Communication Plan throughout the project cycle.

There are, of necessity, tangible differences in roles and responsibilities between the Change Facilitation Team Lead and the project manager for implementation. Consider the story we shared in an earlier chapter in which a company decided to move its headquarters to another location. Traditionally, a project team would be convened and go to work to accomplish the complexities of such a move. With the Adaptive Path, the Change Facilitation Team and the Change Support Network migrate to and becomes a part of the Implementation Team. When you think about it, that makes perfect sense, doesn't it? Why would you drop those with the knowledge about stakeholders from the process and fool yourself that you can still have a people-centric change initiative?

With savvy organizations that think strategically, recognizing the make-or-break reality of support from stakeholders as employees, partners, customers, government entities, and others is foundational.
If you've gotten this far in the book, you understand this concept and acknowledge that the time spent on the human side of the equation will pay huge dividends as change happens.

Kim Leng describes the difference between the two positions in this way:

> The Project Manager is a bit like the father who is task oriented and functions in a disciplinary mode. The Change Facilitation Lead brings in the human element, that maternal mode, that balances the hard and the soft and encourages the Implementation Team to pay attention to how the head and the heart work together.

Strategies for Organizing the Change Facilitation Team

There are a number of viable ways in which the team can be organized. It can morph from the convening management team to the Implementation Project Team. Or the Change Facilitation Team can provide strategic direction while an Implementation Team carries out the day-to-day operation of the change initiative. We believe it would be wise to give the Change Facilitation Team an ongoing role since it will have valuable insider skills based on diverse worldviews as well as an early adaption and commitment to the project.

We promote the core value of dynamic continuity as integral to organizations focused on managing change. Our definition of dynamic continuity demonstrates active involvement over time during which team leaders pass on what they have learned about this Adaptive Path process to others in the organization.

A constant priority is the need to guide the project for maximum effectiveness. Nothing destroys momentum in a change initiative as much as cumbersome processes, missed opportunities and diversions.

We strongly recommended not only diversity of skills and worldviews but also age diversity. Promising young managers bring energy and fresh ideas to the table. They, in turn, learn from more seasoned managers and from the Change Support Network, as individuals the younger ones wouldn't otherwise have been in contact. And finally, of course, these young managers are the leaders of tomorrow. Nothing creates new strengths and perspectives more than being a key player in leading change.

Selecting the Change Facilitation Team members

Essential considerations for team membership include:

- **Select members with diverse perspectives and skills**
  If you are familiar with Edward de Bono's *Six Thinking Hats*, you can consider how that model of operational diversity can strengthen your team. With different perspectives come disagreements. If they are handled as positive exchanges for the greater good, rather than based on the ego of being right, decisions, strategies and implementations will be much stronger because of that diversity.

- **Make certain some of those members have leadership and collaborative roles**
  It is essential that some of the team have experience with projects that require a broader perspective than the procedurally based lead-and-control method.

- **Validate that key members have either initiated the project commitment to the mission and the initiative's goals**
  That doesn't mean team players go along with every idea and have no questions or pockets of resistance. We will continue to remind you that good questions, thoughtfully expressed and clearly fed back to the person who has some discomfort about elements of the initiative, are not only desirable, but also essential.

- **Confirm that team members share important commonalities**
  Strengths include being effective collaborators and having a shared vision along with the integrity to stay the course even when things are not going smoothly. And given the complexity of dynamic change, all of you will

become expert at "becoming friends" with the inevitable nature of change.

- **Focus on the goals of the Change Facilitation Team**
  These include the goals of gathering intelligence, making sense of new learning, and facilitating the change based on the Adaptive Path.

Change Support Network as essential contributors

The members of the Change Support Network have a longer, more diversified relationship with the Change Facilitation Team, acting as the eyes and ears of the assessment of stakeholders during planning, implementation and evaluation.

Many stakeholders could be involved, but only a carefully selected group needs to be central to the process. This group will be invited to be members of the Change Support Network. These key stakeholders will have a strong influence on decision-making and will share responsibility for strengthening the process of following the Adaptive Path in managing the unexpected.

Considerations for selecting your Change Support Network members include:

- Choose people with a tolerance for ambiguity since this process will be new and could feel initially unfamiliar. Their personalities, however, should allow them to handle and be intrigued by these differences.

- Candidates need to have a low tolerance for the usual style of planning.

- It follows that you will be looking for members who believe "ready, aim, fire" is the preferred strategy.

- The colleagues, subordinates, and superiors of those under consideration need to know the candidates are good listeners, with the ability to translate and accurately interpret what they are hearing.

- Candidates need to understand intuitively how pace and magnitude of change impact people in their organization.

- These candidates also need to be able to participate effectively in both planning and implementation.

As Nancy describes it, these networks bring human perspective into the mix.

The Change Support Network will be invaluable in:

- Suggesting stakeholder groups for assessment and analysis
- Bringing ideas to the team for responding to stakeholder concerns
- Sharing rumors and negativity and then suggesting possible responses
- Collaborating with the team on recommendations for the Change Communication and Change Adoption plans

Remember that stakeholders are those who will be impacted by a change initiative and that the Change Support Networks are themselves influencers inside the organization. So on to the story:

> School systems are complicated environments with a high number of stakeholder groups, internal and external. When our consultancy was brought in to consult on a change that impacted thousands of parents, we knew we needed insider assistance.
>
> With input from the client, we recruited a small number of school principals and administrative managers from various regions of the school system so they could translate and inform us about pushback from the major stakeholder group, the parents. The principals were invaluable in translating and informing us about what was happening with the parents as well as being instrumental in pulling them together for a focus group and assisting us in understanding the parent feedback.
>
> This Change Support Network continued to collaborate with us through the entire change initiative, both broadly and specifically. For example, when we were preparing surveys to send out, they provided input on the language and terminology we needed to use to be effectively understood by the parent stakeholders.
>
> Without the Change Support Network, we would have been

> forced to operate from our outsider worldview and that of the schools' senior management. If we had not already been sold on the concept of our Change Support Network, this experience would have made believers of us.

Our recommendation, and one that confirms the importance of its function, is that the Change Support Network should continue to work with the Change Facilitation and Implementation Teams through the entire project. This is an ideal place for us to share a client story that exemplifies how bringing a Change Support Network into the assessment process makes a tangible difference in minimizing resistance to change within the organization.

Selecting stakeholder groups for assessment

Within an organization, management can determine who the stakeholders are, but senior management is not in a position to deal with the nuances at any other level than the telescopic one. To be effective, selecting stakeholder groups for assessment requires zooming down to ground level.

What all this means is that the greater detail you achieve, the better the Change Adoption Plan is, and it follows that the implementation can be more effective. That detail is dependent on selecting the right stakeholder groups for the right reasons. Next you need to gather and take apart this knowledge so it informs what you do, not only with a current change initiative but with future change, both planned and unplanned.

We find it most effective to identify stakeholders by their degree of impact. While identifying and categorizing stakeholders is not entirely scientific, a set of criteria for what constitutes a stakeholder group is helpful. Consider again the organization moving its headquarters. It was easy to determine that this move would most impact staff members. They have less control over their time, tighter schedules with commutes, and family obligations they have to handle. None of these concerns particularly impacts middle and upper management, allowing them to support something that is seen as strategically good for business.

Another example is a situation in which a client, dependent on getting consumer feedback, implemented a Customer Relationship Management system for capturing key customer information. Customers became concerned and began to call customer service in large numbers to register their complaints.

In this case, it's easy to see that the stakeholders most affected are the customer-support representatives. Doesn't it then make sense to get their feedback in solving this problem before jumping to a solution? Because the customer-support representatives are at the tactical, microscopic level and not at the strategic level, they need to be included in problem solving and their frustrations listened to.

Assessment evaluates concerns and readiness

The Readiness Assessment needs to be based on the three types of concern that stakeholders could be experiencing so your team knows how to target these areas. By categorizing these concerns, you are able to more effectively analyze and evaluate the readiness.

We recommend beginning with an in-depth discussion of criteria for assessment. That can be done effectively by conducting a half-day workshop with the Change Facilitation Team and the Change Support Network to lay out stakeholder concerns including their underlying assumptions and beliefs. Make certain you determine the risk if the change initiative isn't properly managed.

This brings us to assessing stakeholder groups most strongly impacted by the change. From there, you need to consider the two dimensions of capability and preparedness as illustrated in the following chart. Readiness to adopt change has two dimensions. One is the level of capability for change, and the other is the level of preparedness for change.

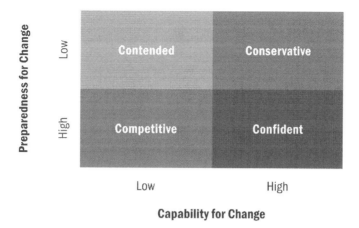

Figure 6 - Stakeholder Readiness Assessment

Because this book is strategic, task-level detail will require our engagement with your process. A team leader's guide and team workbooks will also support this process.

We recommend revisiting these readiness indicators throughout the project implementation so that you can evaluate your efforts at both the micro and macro levels. Some of our clients even post them in their meeting room as visual reminders.

Where do we go from here?

We have considered the complexities and have a high-level understanding of a strategy for evaluating the continuum of both stakeholder readiness and resistance. This is the point where you will "freeze" your findings in order to create the Change Adoption Plan. As the plan is evaluated and implemented, we will move to "unfreeze" mode so we can track the plan's effectiveness and make midcourse corrections where needed.

In our consulting engagements, we act as coaches and "guides on the side." In some cases, you or your organization have only known managing initiatives as command-and-control experiences rather than as an Adaptive Path for managing the unexpected that places people at the center of change initiatives. Authentic decisions about managing change must come from inside the organization.

We continue to refine our Adaptive Path Framework, capturing the knowledge gained from our client engagements. We have been gratified to see evidence that it is working in surprising, often exciting, ways. Our early intuition was correct. But we will never consider the applications of our framework as set in concrete.

As you move from assessment to planning, be keenly aware that support, or lack of it, from management, staff, and a range of outside stakeholder groups makes or breaks an initiative. Even more dramatic, a poorly conceived and executed change initiative leaves a bitter taste in everyone's mouth, and that, of course, makes the next change initiative dramatically more challenging.

In one of Kim Leng's engagements, a European law enforcement senior officer shared a situation with unexpected consequences that dramatically demonstrates what happens when stakeholders are not consulted.

> The police force in a major city installed Global Positioning System-enabled mobile data devices in all its police cars so its officers could always have access to information and track their locations for safety purposes. Management's reasons were valid and well intended. The patrol officers, however, saw it differently. They felt Big Brother was spying on them, tracking them when they took a coffee break or made a stop at home.
>
> In less than a month, all the mobile data devices stopped working. When managers investigated, they were shocked to discover that patrol officers had disabled these devices. In fact, some had not only pulled them out of the car panel but had crushed them as well. You get the picture. Enough said!

This story should have you ready to plunge with us into developing the Change Adoption Plan based on valuable stakeholder feedback you will have collected, assessed, and analyzed.

CHAPTER FIVE
Mapping People-centric Change

Change facilitation planning becomes powerful
when we routinely remind ourselves that it is critical
to base that plan on Awareness, Acceptance, and Adoption.
— Lim Swee Kim, Senior Consultant, KDi

In This Chapter

Rest assured, we aren't proposing reinventing the wheel. All the elements of traditional project planning are firmly embedded in our model. But the method for getting to familiar planning territory is different.

Naming this chapter "Mapping People-centric Change" is not a clever play on words. When you plan a holiday, you identify needs and desires for the journey. Then you start planning and checking in with others to make certain the details work for them. What we are proposing is no different.

Using the Stakeholder Analysis from the assessment cycle, this chapter will empower you and your team to select the most effective strategies for managing the change process. They are the keys to activating success. You will use the Stakeholder Analysis and consult with your Change Support Network before moving to a more familiar systematic planning framework.

From there the focus will be on determining the needs for a Change Communication Plan geared to key stakeholder groups and then integrating the people-centric plan with the Implementation Plan.

Facilitating change through a people-centric process

Did it seem like a long journey to get to this point, where your project manager mode kicks into more familiar territory?

If you have occasionally become impatient that we are almost midway through the book and we have just now begun to focus on planning and implementation, you aren't alone. Your linear brain is a super athlete but the subjects of the first four chapters tap into your emotional brain, an area that doesn't traditionally get much exercise in your workday world.

Take comfort. We are now moving to more familiar territory, but this time with a difference. Stakeholders will remain at the center of the equation. Rather than detract you from the implementation process, they will be skillfully folded into that process. Ideally, the leader for the Change Facilitation Team, who we recommend remains an active and valued member of the Implementation Team, will be the manager.

This people-centric process is like purchasing a racecar. You are familiar with driving a vehicle. You know where things are and expect your trusty sedan to get you to your destination without having to think much about it. But with a racecar, driving is an experience with the unexpected, the excitement and the new skills required to keep that super machine safely on the road while you navigate new, more emotionally based driving experiences.

As we move to the more familiar, mechanical aspects of driving, remember that you are now in possession of a powerful machine, but instead of your usual high-octane gasoline, your fuel is the motivation of your people.

Systematic planning is essential

We recommend going over these ideas with your team at one of your first meetings. Successfully dealing with new ways of thinking and involvement need to be in place from the beginning.

Here are the elements that are the foundation to our systematic planning framework:

- Essential steps need to be planned and implemented as iterative functions so they have a baseline of commonality that increases efficiency and flexibility for modifying particular tasks.

- Managers aren't communication experts, but they are the major communicators up and down the chain, whether for present or future change initiatives. And that's a significant challenge. We're there to coach you through this process. That's why communication techniques and tools are embedded throughout the book. And it's why we will recommend that you bring experts on Awareness, Acceptance and Adoption into your planning sessions.

- The skills of a resilient manager include the traditional skills as well as ones that embrace people skills. Both are necessary to create a plan for change that has a significant chance for success through increased buy-in and Adoption.

Those managerial qualities include:

- Holding a clear vision of what needs to be accomplished
- Paying attention to the logical mind with sensitivity to where resistance happens
- Becoming fully informed about the impending change initiative
- Accepting the need for a migration to a more adaptive way of thinking
- Having inside and outside partners for fresh perspective and expertise
- Committing to change initiatives and to doing what it takes to make the change successful

Steps in change facilitation planning

The change initiative's Change Adoption Plan includes:

- Change Facilitation Strategy
- Change Communication Plan
- Stakeholder Engagement Plan
- Performance Learning Plan

Distilled from our experience gleaned from many projects focused on facilitating change, the following is a time-tested list of our change planning activities:

- Preparing for the change (organizing)

  1. Planning for Change
  2. Establishing Change Facilitation Principles
  3. Mobilizing the Change Support Network

- Understanding the change (analyzing)

  1. Change Analysis
  2. Stakeholder Analysis
  3. Impact Analysis

- Enabling the change (synthesizing)

  1. Defining the Change Adoption Strategy
  2. Creating the Change Adoption Plan
  3. Validating the Change Adoption Plan

Note that if the changes are significant to key stakeholders, all these elements of the Change Adoption Plan will need to be implemented.

Preparing for the change

Before the actual planning starts, the executive sponsor needs to appoint a Change Facilitation Team Lead and select the appropriate members. The team's first steps will be to propose a set of change facilitation principles that will guide the change effort and begin identifying the Change Support Network members

In a sweeping initiative to merge two major local banks in Singapore, we were retained to integrate the operational processes and manage the changes resulting from this merger.

Emotional and assumptive arguments initially dominated the discussions. We facilitated the working groups in finding common ground so they could move directly to the implementation tasks as we continued to remind each group that its job was to create the best processes to meet customer needs.

Every business unit affected by the initiative needs to have representation on the Change Support Network. Sometimes more representatives from one business unit might be on the team if the initiative impacts various roles within the same business units. Carefully selecting these representatives to participant in the planning effort ensures all possible views are considered and creates the support structure from the beginning.

Understanding the change

This is an important activity requiring careful planning by the Change Facilitation Team and the Change Support Network to gather knowledge and sentiments from the various stakeholder groups.

The first step is to draw up a list of known and potential changes required as a result of implementing a change initiative. This step is relatively straightforward since there is always a list of desired changes framed by the need for change or the response to change.

The next step is to conduct a Stakeholder Analysis that significantly involves the Change Support Network. While surveys are efficient, they have many drawbacks. If they are not specific enough, they become a blunt instrument with marginal usefulness. They also have no way of drawing out the follow-up questions that lead to more understanding. Additionally, stakeholders might fear they will somehow be punished if they reveal information that is critical of the organization. We are not opposed to surveys, but we have not found them as useful in these situations as other strategies.

Here's the sequencing we generally recommend for analysis.

Begin by conducting a series of workshops, created to address specific stakeholder concerns brought to the table by the Change Support Network. While workshops are time-intensive for the team, they are invaluable in gathering the context that will lead to effective and innovative change facilitation planning. This strategy demonstrates that feedback from the Change Support Network will result in stronger broad input before a survey is initiated. That survey process provides viable statistical evidence, pinpointing the numbers and the depth of stakeholder concerns and the groups most vulnerable to become resistant to change.

Workshops led by the Change Facilitation Team pull all the evidence together and begin establishing what this process tells you about your stakeholders. Their issues and challenges are documented as concerns and clarifications to ensure they are well understood. All critical concerns are then evaluated through an Impact Analysis that divides them into high, medium and low-impact levels. This process gives both a contextual and critical understanding for the stakeholders' concerns and the impact these concerns might have on the change initiative.

Enabling the change

The first step in this final analysis stage is to anchor the Change Facilitation Team in a broad framework focusing on how to lead the change. Over the years, we have found several strategies to be useful. They can reduce the resistance to and the negative impact of change quite dramatically. Here are some ideas for how these strategies are being used:

- **Identifying a compelling need for change**
  If the change is about survival, it brings a sense of urgency and mobilizes the employees much more effectively. When we worked with organizations that were merged or outsourced, no one questioned the need to pick up new work procedures to stay on the job.

- **Leaders walking the talk**
  For example, when organizational leaders demonstrated they could learn to use e-mail to communicate and coordinate their meetings, the adoption of that communication mode quickly became the norm.

- **Breaking big change into small changes**
  Sometimes, a major change can be daunting. If a significant change, such as adopting a new intranet system – as one of our clients did – is adopted, a more gradual transition can take place as new features are rolled out over several phases. Taking small steps helps people adjust to new work practices and requires less effort as they adapt. They actively remain in both the leadership and learning roles.

- **Using a divide-and-conquer strategy**
  Different groups of stakeholders can adopt change in different stages, depending on the readiness of each group. This practical strategy works

best when the readiness of various stakeholder groups crosses a wide range from resistant to accepting. It allows stakeholders who are more ready to adapt to move faster, but at the same time, it gives additional time to other stakeholders to catch up.

- **Installing quick-wins to create converts**
  In cases where the organization needs to adopt new work practices, a small but successful early adaptation builds confidence and buy-in even for nonbelievers. One of our public-sector clients moved from paper-based case management to electronic case management through quick wins that were built on support and ultimately empowered a long-term successful transition.

- **Providing incentives and support**
  When moving offices to more remote areas, some of our clients have provided new transport arrangements that include accessible pick-up points to reduce the inconvenience experienced by staff. Another client provided food and drink to support staff required to work late.

- **Drawing the line for those who refuse to play**
  Some resistance is more the norm than the exception. After implementing the proactive strategies we recommend, a tipping-point majority should be onboard and ready to adapt to change. For resisters, it might be time to let them know the train is leaving and they have a final opportunity to get onboard.

In the move from assessment to planning, it is critical that the Change Facilitation Team and the Change Support Network participate in workshops with an estimated time commitment of one day per week over a period of three to four weeks. Short meetings with everyone looking at their watches isn't going to give you the essential flow and depth of understanding required for success in the Adaptive Path process. With readiness assessment in place and the commitment by both teams to the process, these workshops establish the framework for creating an effective Change Adoption Plan.

Active, full participation in these workshops ensures valuable discussions that lead to agreement about the change facilitation strategy and plan as well as its contributions to your change initiative.

While the details can be found in the Change Adoption Plan available in Resources, a review of the workshop subjects provides some context for making meaning of a process that is likely to be new to you.

Specifically, the workshops provide the focus and attention for:

- Assessing how to incorporate communication as a key component and how to send its message to key stakeholders including staff and partners.

- Determining how best to engage and involve key stakeholders in clarifying and co-creating the future.

- Designing and delivering learning that speeds the adoption of new skills and insures sustainability.

These three essential concepts will be described and illustrated in detail in Chapters Six, Seven, and Eight, the implementation chapters.

How does this work in real life?

A major Asian university received significant pushback from senior faculty after a change initiative mandated that its faculty teach their classes online. Obviously, a lengthy list of objections came into play, including fear of change, loss of face, and, in the faculty's minds, loss of control. The dramatic shift to online teaching was, understandably, a void, and faculty members had no frame of reference for taking on this new challenge.

The university backed away from the mandate. Instead, it introduced the faculty to using the Internet as a way to expand their thinking and found ways for faculty members to use the Internet for communicating with their students.

Engaging a Change Support Network encouraged some early adapters to experiment, which influenced and encouraged other faculty members to follow suit. Change happens incrementally, always the preferred path for change to stick. It becomes more complicated when change has to happen quickly and impacts multiple stakeholder groups.

In some ways, and because it involves insiders in the process of assessing and bringing a Change Support Network onboard, this phase in any project is like a dress rehearsal for an opening-night theater production. It's an opportunity to work out the process with a friendly group of team members and key stakeholders who support the Change Facilitation Team.

A plan geared to key stakeholder groups

The Change Adoption Plan focuses on the concerns of key groups of stakeholders by minimizing the impact of the transition so they are more likely to adapt to change.

Our methodology, adopted for planning transition and focused on high-impact stakeholder environments, is based on the fundamental stages of Awareness, Acceptance, and Adoption. The plan reinforces strategies for each of the highly interconnected "Three A's" as our Adaptive Path Framework.

We draw heavily on Stakeholder Analysis and Assessment described in this chapter, with specific orientation concerning the individual client's change initiative. This is definitely not a one-size-fits-all approach. All possible ideas go through a rigorous process to determine the strategic and tactical details of a Change Adoption Plan. The design is in response to our unique analysis process that heavily uses input from the Change Support Network. For example, extended activities with a variety of deliveries might be necessary for those stakeholders most heavily impacted, but planning for media coverage might not be much more than a simple press kit widely distributed.

The plan needs to engage select groups of stakeholders through feedback sessions that build commitment and provide opportunities to identify solutions to implementation challenges. For instance, consulting external stakeholders such as parents, in the case of an Singapore Ministry of Education's change initiative, provided superior understanding of their needs and constraints in order to adjust the implementation details. Finally, a performance-driven learning plan, missing in most change efforts, is essential.

Unless learning results in increased performance and an organizational mind-set for continuous education, change cannot take root, and people will gravitate back to old practices. And that leads to frustrations and a build-up of negative perception about the entire initiative.

In most cases, short scenario-based training supported by informal clinic sessions to iron out more specific issues is better than seat time in formal classes. Chapter Eight describes your role and the knowledge you will need to effectively coach and monitor the Adoption process.

Integrating change and implementation plans

The Change Adoption Plan does not exist in a vacuum. In the context of a change initiative, it needs to be woven into the Project Implementation Plan to achieve its greatest impact. The illustration as depicted here highlights how this is accomplished.

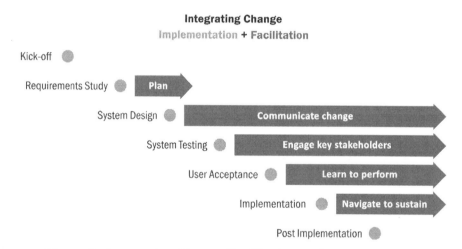

Figure 7 - Integrating Change Facilitation and Implementation

Once the alignment is complete, a more detailed Change Adoption Plan supports the implementation plan.

Change adoption planning is just the beginning

A solid plan ensures you are focused on doing the right things in times of intense change. The questions we ask ourselves to validate an effective Change Adoption Plan are straightforward, but the answers can be more complex. Isn't that just like life?

Questions you might want to ask before finalizing the plan:

- Is there clarity in your vision and outcome for the change?
- Do you have leadership commitment and support?
- Can you build on trust by caring for your people?
- Who and what should you share with your stakeholders?
- What can you do to encourage participation and collaboration?
- How can you improve adoption through performance based learning?

If these questions are considered thoroughly in the Change Adoption Plan, we believe you are on the road to something not just workable but a document that offers your team an "extended warranty" for attaining what you have set out to achieve.

Where do we go from here?

So now it's time to test your planning efforts in the real world with those all-important stakeholders. This is where you will discover in real time how well your own learning curve for people-centric planning plays out during the implementation of the Adaptive Path cycle. We have found that, as in life, important project milestones benefit from conscious acknowledgement and review.

As a culmination of the planning process, we propose a critical reflective exercise that can be highly beneficial. While you have kept the stakeholder concerns in mind, you have focused, correctly, on creating a Change Adoption Plan that is both effective and meets goals.

We suggest your team strongly consider this opportunity to engage the emotive part of your brains with the visioning exercise detailed in the section that follows.

The exercise we are recommending gets everyone's emotional brains firing on all cylinders before you move forward with encounters that you will discover gratify you, perplex you, and possibly even leave you scrambling for higher ground.

You will remember with some fondness the relative calm of understanding the landscape of change, assessing readiness, and crafting strategies for success.

But take heart!

All the times when you felt frustration because you thought you and your team weren't moving fast enough will now pay off. You are likely to say more than once, "Oh, *that's why that step was necessary*" or "*Who would have guessed that the right story could turn around a group of hardcore naysayers?*"

Reflecting on Planning Change

While it is standard business practice to complete a project plan and begin implementation without any reflection, we hope you agree by now that this is not only ill advised: it is falling-off-a-cliff dangerous.

Here's a team reflective exercise we believe will work at multiple levels. In a workshop or retreat setting, have the team consider how they can support and "cross-check" each other throughout the Awareness, Acceptance and Adoption stages.

You can effectively sequence in this way

1. As a whole group exercise, have Implementation Team and Change Support Network members brainstorm all the ways they can support each other.
2. In pairs, they take these ideas and each generates a plan for how they will have touch points that include both the strategic and the procedural. They also identify how they will maximize each other's strengths and take on the challenges of an ongoing relationship.
3. They report back to the group so everyone benefits.

The benefits include

- The pair ideally grows to respect and learn from the other.
- The Change Support Network, probably a new concept in your organization, becomes integrated into the implementation process.
- It offers the advantage of having someone to encourage and expand the other's thinking.
- Their relationship and the feedback sessions to the full group generate ideas for how to improve the pairings and capturing what they are learning for use in future projects.

Leadership Role

Create an awareness of the need for change
Cultivate an acceptance of change
Facilitate the adoption of change

Implementing Sustainable Change

What leaders need to know

Why Implementing Adaptive Change Is Essential

- The three stages of Awareness, Acceptance and Adoption pave the way for sustainable innovation.

- The promise of leading change that matters rests entirely on an active commitment to putting people first.

- In order to achieve sustainability goals, a majority of impacted stakeholders must acknowledge and act proactively to meet the challenges of a change initiative.

- The Change Support Network continues to play an invaluable role getting stakeholders on board and keeping them committed.

Qualities for a Leader Implementing Adaptive Change

- Practice communication as conscious engagement in every stage of implementation.

- Demonstrate leading from the front by being visible, available and accountable.

- Encourage a strongly internalized locos of control for yourself and your team to reach goals and navigate change.

These qualities are particularly important in times of intense planned, as well as unplanned change. Because change is often uncomfortable, people in all levels of your organization will breathe easier if they can sense your confidence and commitment.

CHAPTER SIX
Creating Awareness

Adversity is just change that we haven't adapted ourselves to yet.
— Aimee Mullins, a record-breaker at the Paralympics

In This Chapter

As you prepare to "go live" with your Awareness campaign, your mantra needs to be "reaching out effectively to stakeholders." By the time you finish this chapter, we hope you will join the converted, who now wonder how they ever managed any type of change without making Awareness foundational to their planning, their focus, and their commitment to follow through on the rest of the Adaptive Path.

While stakeholder groups need to be actively involved, you are orchestrating the flow of events at this stage. Later, your team will be collaborating with stakeholders. And, finally, if you are to be successful with change initiatives, the stakeholders move to the driver's seat in the Adoption phase.

However, let's not get ahead of ourselves. As leaders, you need to keep the strategic view and the ultimate positive outcomes clearly in mind. At the same time, you will be actively involved in leading from the front while you and your team execute an Awareness campaign that empowers understanding linked to the stakeholders' willingness to be convinced they can accept change.

Defining Awareness goes beyond the standard definition

Just what is awareness and why is it necessary for getting buy-in for change? Simply put, awareness is when something registers in our brain and stays there long enough for us to remember it.

Our brains, however, are extremely fickle.

If an awareness moment doesn't confirm the question *"What's in it for me?"* the opportunity for a positive awareness, one that sticks with the recipients, is gone. Sadly, that isn't true for holding on to a negative awareness moment. That's why we continue to vividly remember the most embarrassing incidents of our teenage years but not necessarily our successes during that period.

Essential to success, often overlooked

There is a reason we use the term "creating awareness." It doesn't happen automatically, especially because change is too often decided in the boardroom and then announced to line managers and staff members. When that happens, the rumor mill, propelled by fear, often takes over. Instead, you need to consciously create emotionally integrated Awareness campaigns, based on input from the Change Support Network. This will increase the likelihood you achieve that essential tipping point, a key factor in the Adaptive Path to change.

We can't emphasize this too many times: without creating Awareness that appeals to people's positive emotions, any hope of developing Acceptance, let along embracing Adoption, is doomed from the start. Pause and take the time to allow this message to sink in. You will need to internalize these words first so you can sell it to your peers and demonstrate it in all your interactions with highly impacted stakeholders.

Every type of change – from relatively simple event-driven ones to more complex, long-term initiatives – can stumble, and often fatally so, at any stage of the game. And here's another reality check: planning, while absolutely essential, will be easy compared to the implementation phase we are about to explore together. Once buy-in from all except hardcore holdouts becomes central to the change process, you will be grateful you relied on the Change Support Network to provide an insider look at the emotional landscape of key stakeholders.

The use of the word "emotional" is intentional. Like any marketing campaign director, you have one chance to capture the emotions of your stakeholders. And this won't be the last time we will reference marketing as a model for getting the desired positive reactions when a new initiative is introduced. In a broad sense, we market our organization, our mission, and ourselves all the time. Unless we do it authentically and consciously, we are potentially sending negative messages instead of positive ones.

Consulting the experts on Awareness

Bring some of your organization's best marketing people onboard as advisors for your team. Their skills are invaluable throughout the cycle, but particularly in the Awareness phase. Trust us, it will make a difference.

Moving past the traditional Awareness methods

"High tech/low touch" is the traditional way. However, we evolved the concept of "moderate to high touch" for highly impacted stakeholder groups because the traditional method – sending email notices to announce change – doesn't work. But you already know that. We assume you picked up this book, at least in part, because you wanted to adopt more effective ways of engaging people who could make or break your mandate for change.

We hope you now appreciate the Change Support Network's role as the cornerstone of your planning and implementation efforts, but it's natural for all of us to resist change. You might be asking yourself: *"why go to all this effort when we can get the CEO on camera announcing the change, post it on our website, and instruct supervisors to ensure all their people watch it?"* The answer, of course, is that high tech/low touch doesn't work when the goal is capturing stakeholder support through positive emotion.

Later in this chapter, we'll demonstrate how the one-to-many approach can work extremely well when the event includes all the positive elements of high touch. For us, high touch in creating positive Awareness campaigns always means face-to-face interaction. While a teleconference call, followed by relevant updates to a low-impact group that primarily needs access to information, can be sufficient, that strategy is not going to be effective with employees when the change has significant impact on their lives.

Conscious vigilance is critical. Only when you begin implementation with a carefully crafted Awareness plan can you be strongly positioned to achieve the environment in which support grows stronger while resistance weakens.

We recommend you concentrate your efforts on first converting your most highly impacted stakeholders. You will never bring every person onboard, but as first Awareness and then Acceptance gain momentum, the hard-core resisters are left with no one to listen to them except other naysayers.

Communication basics with a difference

The Change Communication Plan focuses on the concerns of key stakeholders and mitigates the impact of the transition so that high-impact groups are more likely to adapt to change.

Our methodology, adopted for planning communication and focused on high-impact stakeholder environments, reinforces strategies for each of the strongly interconnected "Three A's" framework.

In addition to highly impacted internal stakeholders, you might find it necessary to customize your communication approach for strategic partners, vendors, suppliers, customers, selected publics, unions, and media. While overarching communication themes can be used with all stakeholder groups, the strategy used and the style of the message needs to be tailored specifically to each group.

Obviously, focus and depth for dealing with individual groups is project specific. For example, extended activities with a variety of delivery methods might be necessary for those stakeholders most heavily impacted, while planning for media coverage can sometimes be as simple as a press kit widely distributed.

Planning that merges tradition and innovation

Now we will turn to what you often see in books on communication planning. We don't believe in abandoning these principles, but they need to be customized for the Adaptive Path.

In offering new strategies based on emotional buy-in, our intent is to give fresh perspective and then to move on to more tactical communication principles. These principles underpin any successful change initiative, but as you now realize, enabling change can be effective only when you pay attention to the human element.

We are covering these principles here because, while they are essential to the entire implementation process, it's critically important to focus on them at the Awareness stage. We will revisit these principles with specific examples in the Acceptance and Adoption stages.

High-level, strategic principles are always the place to begin. But it's a drastic mistake to assume that posting them on the wall of the team's meeting room is enough. We will be guiding you through a process that allows you to customize each stage of the Adaptive Path to your needs.

Think of these principles listed below as a strategic checklist. Customize it based on your needs, give it culturally specific context, and then use your Change Support Network and Change Facilitation Team to validate and implement your campaign.

- Communicate decisions before you contact stakeholders
- Profile each group of stakeholders
- Communicate proactively
- Target communication to the needs of specific stakeholders
- Ensure all communication includes feedback mechanisms
- Be honest. Communicate the bad news as well as the good
- Ensure communication messages are consistent at every level
- Provide timely information about decisions and events
- Check for understanding through various feedback mechanisms
- Empathize with stakeholders, especially those highly impacted

It's helpful at this point in your journey to review traditional communication planning elements before you move to our Adaptive Path framework: based on utilizing the Change Support Network, this time as interpreters for strategies with potential for a positive response from high-impact stakeholders.

Elements of a traditional communication strategy

- **Develop and define the project**
  As the team lead, you will monitor the primary source of information. Your task is to communicate effectively so you can direct and motivate the project team.

- **Create a forum where ideas can be exchanged**
  Let everyone on the team know his or her contribution is valuable. Communication is a dialogue, and never a monologue. The Change Communication Plan should encourage and model interaction focused on relevant input.

- **Clarify communication goals**
  The goals of good communication should enable the project to be completed effectively and on time. This will help prevent surprises, avoid duplication, and reveal omissions.

- **Steering Committee involved from a strategic perspective**
  This approach is different than the "pure" project management style in which the Implementation Team functions independently on a daily basis. In this traditional model, the Steering Committee deals with elite stakeholders, partners, large customers, government, and other special interest groups. It's easy to see how disconnects happen in this outdated approach.

- **Steering Committee meets less and stays strategic**
  This provides an "intentional pause" to identify lessons learned. It also provides time to make amendments based on feedback from your Change Support Network about how efforts are progressing with the highly impacted stakeholders.

- **Delegate responsibilities**
  Individual members of the Implementation Team should know what their particular responsibilities are and to whom they report. Everyone should know the communication objectives. Use various media and methods to keep communication up-to-date and everyone informed. This includes email updates, project memos, face-to-face encounters, and regular reports on a need-to-know basis.

- **Set a timeline for reports and reviews**
  In addition to the daily exchange of information, also schedule meeting dates and deadlines for reports, a strategy that will keep the team motivated and structured. It also helps to prioritize tasks.

- **Review the Change Communication Plan to ensure it is effective**
  Seek input from the team. *Is the necessary information being communicated in a timely manner? If not, what improvements can be made?*

These classic communication principles are solid, but our experience tells us they will not be sufficient for you to launch and sustain change initiatives. We emphasize that planning is only valuable to the extent it customizes a plan dynamically based on your culture, embedding knowledge about stakeholder needs and the efforts that will prompt them to come onboard.

Now it's time for the caveat. The most excellent plan ever conceived is useless unless it is the backbone for implementation. There are landmines throughout the implementation process. We chose the term "landmines" intentionally. When management steps on a landmine, the damage is immediate, and the collateral damage must be dealt with decisively and proactively. Anticipate as many of these landmines as possible and be proactive in rectifying what is not working.

> **Use your Change Support Network as the human detectors**
> for finding those landmines before they explode.

Creating Awareness campaigns is an inside job

Change initiative's strategies must emerge from the planning stages, internalized and led by the Change Facilitation Team. Our role with clients is to engage them, inspire them, and assist them with strategic focus. Just like a stage manager, we believe our role is a behind-the-scenes effort to help you, the primary players, translate your Awareness Campaign goals into an enthusiastically received Acceptance phase.

If you depend on external consultants for other than a collaborative coaching role, you are handing over your power to outsiders who understand marketing but not the powerful nuances of what makes your organizational culture tick. The end result can be polished and catchy, but it will be missing the integrity and passion only insiders can provide at the inception of a change initiative.

However, after you are clear about the strategy and methods for your campaign, don't be afraid to call in outside help, including graphics illustrators, webmasters, and others with specific skills you lack internally.

As you work with contractors, we encourage you to trust your reaction and that of your Change Support Network to ensure their concepts resonate.

We recommend that our clients test each communication campaign with a small group of trusted stakeholders, giving the campaign a trial run before it goes public. We think this is a wise thing to do before you run the risk of putting on a campaign that management believes is pitch perfect but might die a slow, painful death after it goes public with high-impact stakeholders.

This bears repeating: just as in traditional marketing, you have only one chance to make a good impression. Second chances come at a high price and usually require heavy equipment to pull the project out of the hole that management has dug for itself.

Make creating ideas that stick a priority

We'll refer frequently to the term "stickiness" in this section of the book. We believe in the concept so deeply that we recommend you buy copies of the book *Made to Stick* for your team. It is chock-full of suggestions for reinforcing the essential role of emotional messages that resonate.

Ideas that stick are always congruent with your geographical culture as well as your organization's culture. Emerging countries have an advantage because they are closer to their cultural heritage as a way of life. That is particularly true where the power of story comes into play.

Terms such as "stickiness" and "tipping point" call up strong visual images. Keep in mind that themes must prompt people's individual interpretation as a personal story or emotion. The human brain can take a snippet of music, a single image, or simple animation and create a personalized version of the story. Once stakeholders have done that with a tagline, a theme, or a story, they "own" it, a sure sign the Awareness campaign is effective. That doesn't mean you have won the battle, but you have their attention in a positive way. The Change Support Network and employee supervisors need to monitor situations in which groups of high-impact stakeholders may have misunderstood the intent of the Awareness campaign.

And, of course, within any organization there are diverse subcultures based on multiple factors including ethnicity, age, gender, and educational background. We strongly recommend you pay attention to those differences, not just for a current campaign but also as a foundational value for the way you sustain and grow your business.

Adaptive Path methods for engagement

The right story, visual element, or theme must speak a universal language with your stakeholders, both internal and external. By this, we mean that these elements must be positively and emotionally meaningful so people can move from Awareness to Acceptance. This is an important distinction. In normal business mode, different levels in an organization think differently and communicate within that difference. This is a challenge for the messengers. They might need to consciously step out of their normal operational style to be effective with others. This is particularly true when you move from the strategic-communication style of leadership to the concrete style of line staff.

We agree with Rosabeth Moss Kanter, a professor of business administration at Harvard, who says branding a concept involves three principles including:

- Clear, memorable, succinct messages are the foundation of a change campaign. Create a message that is emotionally compelling and easily repeated.

- People remember stories better than numbers or facts. Tell stories about why the change is important or illustrate the benefits of changing.

- For any campaign to be successful, the audience needs to know what it can do. Be clear about the action you want your people to take and the ways they can start to help immediately.

For each of the implementation stages, we recommend planning strategically and then populating a grid where you carefully identify needs, highly impacted stakeholders, delivery systems, and methods for evaluating the strategy.

This shouldn't be done superficially. It is your road map. It incorporates input from the Change Support Network, your link to stakeholders. In addition to considering each category separately, make certain the delivery choices have a logical, dynamic flow to increase that all-important awareness factor.

Concepts for rolling out your Awareness campaign

Successful initiatives need to include all these components:

- Get stakeholder attention through the unexpected.
- Increase understanding by making messages concrete.
- Make your communication credible by believing what you say.
- Ensure stickiness by caring passionately about the message.
- Use stories to demonstrate the power of your commitment.

Change Communication Plan

The grid below evolved from our reflective dialogues and has been validated through our client engagements. While the broad delivery choices are what we strongly believe are essential to success at this stage, how and in what form you use them are decisions only you and your team can make, based on factors specific to your situation.

And keep in mind that all your Change Communication Plan choices are foundational. They will have primary or supporting roles as you move through the Adaptive Path cycle.

When the Need Is	Impacted Stakeholders	Effective Delivery Choice	How Choice Addresses Need	Evaluating Intervention Effectiveness
Providing current and pertinent information	Everyone is impacted	**Strategy** to reinforce other delivery choices	Every stakeholder receives their information personalized to job function	Identify if stakeholders are getting what they need with compelling and accurate communication
Making message believable and compelling	Everyone from the CEO to the custodian benefits	**Branding** Using metaphors as taglines	The right logo and phrase has the power to unite, rather than divide	Change Support Network monitors Awareness levels

When the Need Is	Impacted Stakeholders	Effective Delivery Choice	How Choice Addresses Need	Evaluating Intervention Effectiveness
Capturing imagination: identifying with stake-holders	Highly impacted groups, inside or outside the company	**Story Telling**	Helps stakeholders understand what's in it for them	Note whether elements of the story show up in employee conversation
Gathering and using feedback from stakeholders	Utilizing Change Support Network	**Feedback Sessions**	Confirms active listening	Changes folded into key messages
Honoring stakeholder concerns	Highly impacted and most vulnerable	**In Person Sessions** **with Upper Management**	Respects stakeholders by validating their concerns	Team member debriefs management on stakeholder concerns
Latest and most accurate information tailored to specific subgroups	High-impact stake-holder groups	**Continuous Delivery** "FAQs" Newsletters Project website	Shows transparency and trust	Evaluates how well these modes accomplished their purpose

Communicating with a difference during change

Asking the important questions:

- Who needs your information to become aware of the change?
- What expectations do you want to set?
- How much information do you need to disseminate?
- How often do you need to disseminate?
- How do you ensure consistency in communication?
- Which communication channels do you need to use?

Each stakeholder group is unique

Borrowing from successful marketing campaigns that always begin a new campaign by gathering relevant data, we recommend you have your team creates a profile of each stakeholder group.

A successful demographic profile starts with general truisms about employees, based on their job description. But you don't need to, and shouldn't, stop there. Remember that your Change Support Network has representatives from every department. Recruit them to customize the general demographic profiles. Drilling down with data about your own employee culture can be extremely beneficial, now and as a future baseline.

Different stakeholder groups have different needs that are defined by their roles and involvement. For example, they could be grouped according to relevant job functions, level of authority for decision-making, or customer relationships.

Setting clear expectations

- What are the issues?
- What will change accomplish with respect to goals?
- How will issues create problems, if unaddressed?
- What is the rationale behind each suggested change?
- What is the decision-making process?
- Who are the key players responsible for the change?
- What is the optimal timing for feedback and comments?

Key questions as you plan for kickoff

- Do you have the right message?
- Is the right messenger delivering the message?
- Are you using effective multiple channels for delivery?
- Are you repeating your message multiple times?
- Is face-to-face communication honored and acted upon?
- Does the message have appeal to all impacted stakeholders?
- If not, then how do you personalize the key message?

Try a new way that's different from what you've always done

And, finally, strategies should never be chosen simply because "that's the way we do it here." Wipe that slate clean, and take a fresh look at absolutely everything. "This gives you the opportunity to determine how puzzle pieces fit together," Nancy points out, "and what that means to choices concerning your essential message, the best messenger to deliver that message, and the delivery channel for optimal delivery."

Managing communication strategically 24/7

There is a strong relationship between an individual's receptivity to change and the quality of the communication about the initiative. You need to begin with a strategic communication approach, follow through with strategies that increase an environment for positive emotional response, and back up your efforts using the 24/7 capabilities of digital communication. This backup should be constantly monitored and modified, based on the feedback your team is collecting from stakeholders.

Benefits of people-centric communication

- Clarifies in order to understand vision
- Reduces resistance to change and results in a better-informed workforce collaborating to achieve the benefits of change
- Unifies teams that pull in the same direction
- Offers an interactive framework for continuing communication
- Reinforces positive messages that support goals

Gauge communication levels

- Too much information leads to confusion and irritation
- Accurate and timely information is key
- Repeat messages via multiple channels, for maximum impact
- Tailor communication to the needs of the stakeholder groups

Monitor communication consistency

- Misinformation is more common than you think
- Minimize misinformation by responding quickly to rumors

- Communication content/messages need to have a consistent style and be presented in straightforward, concise language
- The project committee should centrally manage dissemination

The new face of branding: reconsider how it can work for you

Isn't branding something marketing people do to get you to buy things you don't need? Perhaps, but branding is emotionally powerful and has integrity if you use it consciously and for the common good.

Seth Godin, an author and online marketing expert, reminds us that a brand used to be a logo or a design but has morphed into something more contextual. "A brand's value is merely the sum total of how much extra people will pay," he says, "or how often they choose, the expectations, memories, stories and relationships of one brand over the alternatives."

While we find the new face of branding congruent with our philosophy, there is still a place for using its traditional concept. When you think about a global brand such as, say, Apple, the now-famous image for its family of products immediately comes to mind. If your organization has a visual brand or a tagline like Apple's "think outside the box," use it to help your campaign. One of our Singapore clients, the Ministry of Manpower, refers to its employees internally as "MOM-ers", so when the ministry engaged us to assist with the deployment of an integrated filing-and-exchange system, it was natural to use their cartoon mascot as a visual reinforcement.

Before you consider using your organization's brand as the basis for creating a theme for your change project, ask yourself:

- Does our brand have a track record and credibility?
- Is it a message that is "sticky" and has a long shelf life?
- Will the message resonate with the most impacted and the most important stakeholder groups?
- Does the theme lend itself to multisensory applications? In other words, can it tell a visual story, recognizable to everyone?
- Can you imagine stakeholders adapting the tagline or the abbreviation into their language when they talk about the project?

And even if you don't choose to go public with your brand, it can keep the team focused throughout the planning and implementation cycles.

An extension of branding as a strategy is identifying a theme that is relevant, simple, and will resonate with a particular stakeholder group. For example, if your company is moving to a new location and you want to get the support of your employees, you might use a theme such as "We're Moving House".

The highest impact stakeholders will be your employees. Since they are all householders, they will be able to identify immediately how this will impact them personally. Later in the chapter, we will share with you the story of how one company brought this thematic tag line to life.

Stories give life its emotional meaning

If you and your team can craft a powerful, relevant story and use it in a variety of ways, you will be well on your way to reaching people at their emotional core.

Stories aren't just for children. The ability to tell, hear, and make meaning of stories is one of the attributes that makes us human. Over the millenniums and long before people traveled or knew of other lands, stories were the bedrock of every culture. As it turns out, it doesn't just drive culture. Roger Schank, a cognitive scientist, and others in his field have demonstrated that our brains make meaning of the world through story. Even a single word tells a story if it has meaning for the speaker and the listener.

Nancy has powerful memories of an effective story she heard years ago.

> In the mid-1990s, when I was living in Asia, a world-class knowledge management conference took place in Singapore. It was heady stuff, and all the sessions were packed. One of the keynote speakers, an American academic, told a story about crocodiles in the sewers of Singapore as an analogy for assuming that information we can access readily is entirely different from the mind-sets that splash around in the sewers of our unconscious. Asian audiences can be tough, but this speaker had this one spellbound.

On at least three occasions at other gatherings over the next few years, she heard that story repeated, and the person would inevitably ask how an American was able to tell such a powerful story about Singapore.

We believe this storyteller was able to transcend cultural differences by querying locals about myths and cultural icons. He knew the point he needed to make to capture his audience and went in search of a compelling story to support it. We can do no less when it is imperative that we capture the minds and hearts of our stakeholders

Nancy doesn't remember who the speaker was, but she does remember the story and that's what stickiness is all about. That storyteller did his homework, and it grabbed the audience! What does this have to do with implementing a Change Communication Plan? The short answer is "everything." The right story or image speaks strongly to multiple audiences.

Use metaphor to guarantee stickiness

Steven Covey, a college professor and the author of *The Seven Habits of Highly Effective People*, was a master of the power of expressive language, and used metaphors about humans to guarantee stickiness. In doing so, he made a powerful statement about the challenge faced in capturing the positive emotional response needed from employees.

In his book, *The 8th Habit*, Covey describes a poll based on interviews with 23,000 employees from diverse companies.

- "Only 37 percent said they had a clear understanding of what their organization was trying to achieve and why.
- Only one in five was enthusiastic about the goals of his/her team and organization.
- Only one in five said he/she had a clear 'line of sight' between his/her tasks and the team's organizational goal.
- Only 15 percent believed their organization enabled them to execute goals.
- Only 20 percent fully trusted the organization they worked for. "

This is a cold dose of reality but still abstract. Consider how these statistics come alive when Covey uses those same numbers in the context of a soccer match.

> If a soccer team has these same scores, only 4 of the 11 players on the field would know which goal was theirs. "Only 2 of the 11 would care. Only 2 of the 11 would know what position they play and know exactly what they are supposed to do. And all but 2 of the players would, in some way, be competing against their own team members rather than the opponent."

Feedback sessions as a powerful tool

Feedback sessions are useful in drawing out stakeholder concerns. The facilitator listens, asks guiding questions, and feeds back concerns for agreement or clarification. We believe that listening to and responding to stakeholders and feeding their comments back to upper management is absolutely essential.

These facilitators need to consciously step out of their normal operational style to be effective with others. This is particularly true when they are moving from the strategic communication at the top of the organization to the concrete style used by employees who are centered on that familiar issue of self-interest.

Stakeholder sessions with upper management: it starts at the top

It's not about strategies that are supposed to work. It's about getting at the core of evolving communication issues and demonstrating flexibility muscle by responding decisively with all the emotional intelligence you and your team can muster.

The initiative can fail because it's not supported from the top, and it can fail because it's not supported from the bottom.

We have found in our client relationships that communication with different groups can often be a difficult leap, but with coaching in a collegial environment, management can become comfortable with, and even feel good about shaping change through authentic conversation. It might be helpful to remind yourself that you already seamlessly manage communication-style differences in your personal life.

You are the same essential person with your neighbor, your mother-in-law, and your children. But the communication style is different in each of your relationships.

Digital delivery geared to key stakeholder groups

In defining its communication strategy, we have identified and widely tested these key principles:

- Changes must be communicated beforehand and as specifically as possible. The more drastic the change, the more lead-time is necessary for people to absorb the change.
- Communication must always start with stakeholders within the organization and should be followed by communication with external stakeholders.
- Feedback and suggestions on dealing with changes by various stakeholders are actively sought, and all actions are to be communicated back to the relevant stakeholders.

You need to:

- Give internal stakeholders the high-level calendar of events and Change Communication Plan prepared for external stakeholders.
- Provide briefing materials and Frequently Asked Questions (FAQs) on various project transition stages as well as answers to common queries.
- Actively seek feedback from stakeholders in updating FAQs.
- On a periodic basis, update all materials, place them on the corporate intranet, and make them available to stakeholders.

Remember that newsletters, FAQs, and fact sheets should never be considered a primary means of effectively getting stakeholders onboard and committed.

However, having correct information available 24/7 can keep the rumor mill and "arm-crossing" at a minimum.

If a contentious issue arises, these delivery channels are not effective. Therefore we never recommend them as an appropriate response to polarizing situations. But they have a place in your tool kit of strategies if they are kept dynamic and responsive.

People lead with their emotions,
then move to their logical side once they are onboard.

Newsletters are typically filled with short stories and anecdotes, and they are often published on a regular basis. Electronic versions have gained popularity in recent years, but remember it is tempting to delete them when they are delivered by email. We find it more effective to post newsletters on the intranet's project website as articles or to download the newsletter so an individual can choose when and in what form it is read. If the newsletters are well designed and eye catching, they can be posted at locations where employees regularly gather for updated information.

A strategy for making FAQs relevant and powerful

FAQs are concise answers to questions on a particular subject. Audiences are expected to read through FAQs before asking further questions. The FAQs provide self-help for people who are new to a specific area of knowledge or project.

What's missing here? Have you lost count of the times you tried to get an answer about your online banking or a product you purchased only to find the FAQs extremely frustrating and probably useless for solving your problem? How can you avoid this? Instead of having an editor who is isolated from the highly impacted stakeholders, ask your Change Support Network and the stakeholders' supervisors what they believe will be the most frequently asked questions. Then give someone the responsibility for updating those questions and responding to them based on engagement and feedback. To emphasize, information that is always available online is a reinforcement, not a replacement, for face-to-face communication.

Fact sheets need to be short, relevant, and answer a single question

Fact sheets break down complicated information into more digestible pieces. Individual sections of the sheet are frequently captioned to guide the reader to a specific section. When several subjects need to be covered, you should create separate fact sheets.

Good fact sheets will help you avoid creating multiple letters or giving long explanations on the phone. The information provided needs to be clear and consistent.

An innovative Awareness campaign for high-impact stakeholders

We suggest you read this section twice, and the second time, note why you think it could be effective, risky, innovative, or possibly all three. It will be interesting to compare your observations with our notes below the campaign description. You might also want to consider sharing it with the Implementation Team when it evaluates how leadership will announce a change initiative that impacts the rank and file.

Remember the company that decided to move its manufacturing plant? It sent a memo to all its employees and then got busy planning the move. Imagine the rumors, the grumbling, and the negativity that swept through the company as the moving date approached.

But what if the CEO had convened a Change Support Network with a representative from each of the company's departments? Here's what might have happened in this fictitious event:

This network provided input to design a Change Communication Plan based on helping the employees deal proactively with the move. The theme selected was a single tagline: "We're Moving House." People could identify with this concept because most would have experienced such an event in their personal lives.

The CEO also called a general meeting to make an announcement about the move. People arrived both curious and nervous. The CEO sat on the stage with a mike. His posture and attitude expressed inclusion and trustworthiness to the audience.

"We have determined we need to move the plant to a new location," the CEO said. This is similar to the times you've moved from one home to another. Our move requires us to consider its pros and cons. It will be disruptive for a while, but it will give us room to grow and easier access to our customers. And when we thrive, your jobs are more secure.

While we know it might create complications in your personal life as you make adjustments, for example, in commuting to work, we want to make it as easy as possible for you. So we have set up a Change Support Network. Someone from your department is on that team.

If you look around, you will see that person holding a large sign with the name of your department on it. Follow that person, and you will arrive in a room where lunch is waiting. Over lunch, you will be asked to come up with suggestions for what would make the move easier and more efficient. All the suggestions will be considered. Senior management will choose the department with the best suggestions, and everyone in that department will be given an extra day's paid leave over the next year.

Before we start operations at the new plant, we will have a celebration. You and your family will be our honored guests, and our company will provide entertainment, good food, and music. You can explore all the facilities, including my office, and take a look, with your family, at the area where you will be working.

This move is going to make our business stronger. But the most important strength of our business is each of you.

Enjoy your lunch, come up with your best ideas, and then talk to your supervisor if you need assistance with complications caused by the move. A year from now, when we have been in the new location long enough to get settled in, we'll have another celebration."

What elements of a quality plan are embedded in this example?

The CEO delivers a targeted, respectful message, and then turns the meeting over to supervisors whom he sees as the most effective group to mentor and motivate the company's teams and the group most available for questions and concerns. Notice how the CEO wove in reassurance and validation. Concerns were acknowledged and then incentives were offered. And people had an immediate opportunity to talk about and be involved in problem solving the challenges of "moving house".

You will probably agree with us that this approach is an excellent script for the occasion. But at the end of the day, it's the sincerity and integrity of the CEO that will make or break this communication approach.

When an announcement is done well it is too often interpreted as a success. Instead, it is simply a successful beginning. While the project described above is fairly straightforward – it has a finite goal and is event driven rather than process driven – it could be a dismal failure. Consider the fallout if employees discover their suggestions are never acted upon or if the celebration at the new facility is poorly planned and executed.

The company could find itself with a new facility peopled by disgruntled, poorly motivated employees.

Remember you are first seeking Awareness and then Acceptance for a plan that needs primary stakeholder support to succeed, and that involves not only committing to, but also delivering on its promises.

You and your team need to constantly understand more, and care more, about strategic direction. To market your vision successfully, you will have to be sincerely respectful and attentive to your employees, people who have a decidedly more concrete agenda than you do for why they will decide – or won't decide – to support innovation.

So how would you prep your Managing Director on a presentation about the proposed change?

Here is a simple abbreviation that synthesizes Awareness pitched to capture emotions:

- **B**rief
- **R**espectful
- **I**nteresting
- **M**atters

Is there risk in this innovative approach to this strategy? Absolutely, but there is a greater risk of failure if you resort to the high-tech, low-touch approach rather than modeling innovation. Is this approach that we've presented here for everyone? Clearly, the answer is no. Using the strategies we recommend, your team will be able to execute an Awareness campaign grounded in an emotionally congruent style that fits your organization's culture.

Where do we go from here?

Our framework has three distinct phases to help you avoid the prospect of missing the opportunity to capture positive emotional support for your change initiative at its inception. And let's be clear. If you miss that opportunity before the well is poisoned with rumors and criticism, you probably won't have the chance to capture that momentum again.

While you will already have worked out the strategies and the details of the Change Communication Plan, we recommend you implement your well-crafted follow-up plan in the Acceptance phase so you can concentrate on Awareness as a separate process.

In moving from Awareness to Acceptance to Adoption, the key ingredient is the ability to internalize and act on the elemental truth that, at the end of the day, it's all about communication as continuous feedback and respectful, authentic response to that feedback.

There is no clear line you need to draw between the cycles of Awareness and Acceptance. Strategies and delivery methods can begin in Awareness and be reinforced in Acceptance.

The critical thing to remember is this: you usually have only one opportunity with employees to create a receptive environment for tilting the fulcrum in your favor. That doesn't always mean a single event, but it does mean a conscious, decisive, and possibly bold Change Communication Plan based on creating positive emotions.

While your vendors, your strategic partners, and your own management team want a bottom line, straight answers, and knowledge specifically targeted to each of these groups, it's always about first capturing the emotion with internal, highly impacted stakeholders.

CHAPTER SEVEN
Cultivating Acceptance

I've learned that people will forget what you said, people will forget what you did,
but people will never forget how you made them feel.
— Maya Angelou, poet and novelist

In This Chapter

We have covered some dense territory to reach this point, much of it possibly new to you or presented in a way you haven't considered before. Because we believe truly innovative ideas can be expressed simply without sacrificing their contextual complexity, we will offer some simple but powerful strategies that focus on your stakeholders' needs.

At this point, and if you have crafted your Awareness phase well, many of your stakeholders have uncrossed their arms, become more open, more clearly aligned, and, at a minimum, are now willing to consider why the organization needs to make changes.

We will also focus on changing hearts as a fundamental issue of commitment. This is the point in our journey where people make a firm decision to get onboard. Only after changing attitudes and making commitment is it possible to begin to change behavior, a topic we will explore in Chapter Eight.

Defining Acceptance

Acceptance occurs when people internalize the need for change and are open to considering a long-term arrangement. If Awareness is like a first date, Acceptance is deciding to be a couple, and Adoption is making a long-term commitment.

To be open to that ultimate commitment, people need to know how the planned change applies to them. You will win more hearts and minds if the strategies you use are relevant to individuals. We will be recommending a number of ways you can deepen Acceptance so Adoption doesn't seem like a huge step, but instead, is a natural progression to the next level.

Bringing stakeholders onboard

The goal at this stage is to develop commitment based on stakeholder values, building trust through extensive interactive communication that result in a sense of community and shared vision. As is true with the entire change process, it's about conscious communication in an atmosphere that values people by respecting individuality, treating people fairly, and being open to their ideas and suggestions.

This extends quite naturally to the relationships among senior management as well as the Implementation Team. If you do not have absolute transparency and a commonality of mission at the top, your internal and external stakeholders will have adverse emotional reactions to the plan. While they are likely to forgive well-intended mistakes if you admit you made them, they will not forgive anything that feels like deception or lack of respect.

While this chapter offers solid ideas concerning *what, when, where, why*, and *how* strategies for capitalizing on the positive feelings generated during the Awareness phase, no events or feedback sessions, however well they are done, will be successful unless your leadership truly leads by example.

Conscious communication is the key to conversion

This is the juncture in the change cycle when you have your stakeholders' attention and where you need to expand and deepen the channels of communication. Nothing is more disheartening than getting your stakeholders' attention and then missing effective implementation by failing to pay attention to conscious communication. It doesn't matter how many ways you deliver your message. If you don't get to the heart of the matter, all your effort will be useless.

We use two simple, effective communication models for the Acceptance stage of our client work. We strongly encourage you to take some time to reflect on their meaning and then share them with your Implementation Team and Change Support Network so they can manage an effective sequencing of real-time events and delay-time delivery systems that result in readiness for behavioral change.

You might want to bookmark this and come back to it with a cup of coffee, saving it until you have the opportunity to consider how the models encourage tipping-point levels with your stakeholders.

Achieving success through authentic engagement

The commitment-based approach rather than the control-based approach becomes essential as you implement the Acceptance stage of this framework. To build commitment, you must move away from a control-based traditional approach where work environments are viewed as static. To assume that you can control the emotional responses of people or the chaotic nature of change, either in your own communities or in the world, is, to put it plainly, an utter fantasy. While it is human nature to want to control your environment, you will be more successful and experience less stress if you embrace the commitment approach. Your organization might well be littered with well-intended, poorly communicated change initiatives from management who believe the top-down controlled method gets the job done.

In a dynamic environment where change is coming fast and furious, you need to build trust and a sense of community so that people embrace the change from their hearts and make choices that lead to Adoption. This leads to more conscious communications as authentic engagement by offering compelling reasons for key stakeholders to participate in becoming active participants. The strategies we use and recommend to our clients mirror this commitment-based approach.

At this juncture, the initiative can fail because it's not supported from the top or the bottom. Our philosophy is that the dynamic of listening to and responding to stakeholders and then feeding their concerns to upper management is absolutely essential. Once again, the importance of a fully engaged Change Support Network, that is listened to and included in decision-making, is essential.

Attention to the problem is not the answer

A proactive response to change and innovation is the opposite of problem solving. If you get trapped in the rigid, reactive mode of attempting to fix problems that, of course, never stay fixed, you are stuck in an increasingly vicious cycle. Instead, all your efforts must be focused on using strengths to shore up underdeveloped areas that might be holding you back; instead consistently focusing on solutions rather than problems.

Can we agree now that there is a fundamental difference in the way our brains respond to people dynamics when we view them as a challenge instead of as a problem? Being presented with a challenge gives us a legitimate sense of empowerment, while being handed a people problem to fix registers as negative in our "emotional" brains. That's a bad idea in every respect.

Since it's not just a planning group, the network should be consulted in rolling out campaigns, focus groups, and other activities during the implementation. Olivier Serrat, the head of the Knowledge Management Center at the Asian World Bank, synthesizes the importance of facilitating positive change with a basic, uncomplicated assumption: every organization has things that work well. Serrat identifies Appreciative Inquiry as "an exciting generative approach to organizational development" and believes at a higher level it is also a way of being and seeing.

Does the term Appreciative Inquiry strike you as one of those "soft" initiatives? As we have delved into the fundamentals of this approach, we have found it deeply congruent with our own Adaptive Path philosophy. We have validated that this framework succeeds remarkably well with clients and is a powerful method for guiding groups to refocus on their organization's positive aspects.

As you read through the underlying principles of Appreciative Inquiry, think back to the last chapter in which we focused on the necessity of paying attention to your employees, including their fears, their desires, and their stories. These are the foundations of any successful change initiative. Serrat has accurately identified some basic tenets of human nature.

Your Implementation Team can reach its own tipping point and be substantially more effective with stakeholders if they embrace these points:

- Organizations are not machines.

- Organizations are social realities constructed between people.

- Important organizational processes – including communicating, decision making, and managing conflict – hinge more on how the people involved make meaning out of their interactions and less on the skillful application of techniques.

It will be valuable to consider this framework precisely in terms of the change initiatives that will involve you directly.

Keeping your team and yourself energized and focused

So far we have focused on the process, the philosophy, and the project management aspects of selling your change initiative. It is essential that you stay tuned in to your team and monitor your own internal landscape during this journey we have undertaken together. Much of the Adaptive Path underpinnings might be new to you. That brings with it both excitement and nervousness about having significant responsibilities that stretch comfort zones.

You might want to watch for signs in yourself and others concerning a shift in the way you believe and engage. Such shifts can either be stressful or exciting, depending on the individual's personality. Practicing the art of conscious communication and collaboration within the team is good rehearsal for working effectively with stakeholders that empowers consensus decision-making.

Most of us view our business and personal lives either as a series of projects or as an open-ended journey. You will likely have both perspectives on your team. And that makes for the perfect storm because managing projects without vision leads people in circles, while visionaries tend to strike out on a path without initiating the steps it takes to achieve important goals.

It's important to play to the strengths of your team just as you need to do with your stakeholders. Members of your team need to "own" their roles in order for it to become second nature. This ownership needs to be balanced by authentic collaboration, honoring what others do well in alliance with the strength of one's own contribution. This sets up an environment in which each team member sees a successful journey as more compelling than the reactive response of retreating into control mode.

Organizing a retreat day

At this stage, you and your team need to pause in preparation for moving into the fast-paced activity of the Acceptance stage. Here, you need to use thoughtful consideration and then action-oriented refinements as your guide. This is what we believe is an ideal strategy for you to use before beginning the Acceptance stage. Plan a retreat day for your team. At the retreat, give time and attention to the questions below. They are important and should not be considered while the demands of a regular workday distract you and your team.

- Is the Implementation Plan you and your team created meeting the goals you had intended?

- What do you now know that you didn't know before you moved from planning to implementation?

- Are those goals still consistent with your vision, or has what you learned in the Awareness stage altered what you now believe are your goals?

- Has your Change Communication Plan met its goals?

- How does that analysis of the Change Communication Plan impact decisions you are making at this stage?

- You are moving into the stage where you will need conscious and consistent communication with your stakeholders as well as feedback from them. What does that tell you about the strategies you are about to implement?

- Does your Implementation Plan give evidence that you can reach a tipping point for Acceptance that will make possible behavioral changes in the Adoption stage?

Even if you need to have dinner delivered to the meeting space, we recommend you don't leave until everyone has reached consensus on decisions and how those decisions will play out. Then arrange for team members to have a half-day off their regular schedule to individually consider the consensus results of the retreat day. Finally, have a meeting of no more than two hours in which final agreements are confirmed, and the team has its action plan.

And remember to applaud what has been accomplished. You made it successfully through the Awareness stage and gained some ground. There have been times when you and others might have wondered why it was worth all the effort. You have confirmed that putting people first really does work. Things will move quickly in this phase. Executed skillfully and with good intent, you and your team are going to feel as if you just won a national championship when you get to the analysis stage for your Acceptance game plan.

Evolution to Acceptance needs to be seamless to stakeholders

In reality, any delay as you move toward implementing Acceptance will weaken your efforts. The last thing you need is to lose the advantage of the stickiness you have achieved for selling the basic concepts to your highly impacted stakeholder groups.

As we have pointed out in our recommendations for successful Awareness campaigns, there is no hard line where one phase ends and another begins. This step must be seamless so the Stakeholder Engagement Plan rolls out immediately in order to advantage traction for positive changes in attitude.

Ideally your highly impacted stakeholders are not aware you are now implementing the second stage of the Adaptive Path Framework. The reality for where you are and where you need to go resides exclusively with your Change Facilitation Team, especially the representatives from the Change Support Network.

This is the most effective way to use the Adaptive Path concepts as a strategy for making sense of what you are doing. We recommend the terms Awareness, Acceptance, and Adoption never be used in your communication with your stakeholders. This does not in any way signal lack of transparency. People want to be convinced and to be involved because of what's in it for them. Pause for a moment and acknowledge that if the situation were reversed and one of the company's external partners had a new initiative they were rolling out, you might find yourself with some resistance based on the impact that partner's initiative has on you.

This is no different than a group of engineers who have their own language but need to communicate to people outside the field, including their bosses and the company's customers, about how new technology-driven change will benefit stakeholders. Those groups don't care how the technology is being developed. They only care how it will impact them. You might be thinking that's just common sense. But all of us, no matter how skilled we are as communicators, sometimes fall into the "everyone-should care-as-much-as-I-do" trap. We routinely, and unconsciously, communicate from our subject-matter-expert perspective rather than from the customer or stakeholder perspective.

Tommy Cheung Chi King, a Singaporean who worked in Europe, Middle East and Africa for eight years and currently in Asia Pacific, is a senior consultant with an engineering background and is the sales lead for a major corporation selling high-end software solutions to the global banking industry. He explains it this way: "I never take communications for granted. While I am the subject-matter expert about the technology we sell, I communicate with clients in terms that make sense to them, making certain my approach is very conscious and always focused on the needs and motivation of the client."

We all need to pay attention to his observations about what is required to morph from one role to another, in his case, from engineer to sales lead where he is managing those two world-views successfully.

Whether it is staff, middle management, external/internal partners, vendors, or large groups such as the Singapore Ministry of Education's change initiative involving thousands of parents, change is successful because stakeholders are consulted, listened to, and, wherever possible, their concerns addressed.

We have covered the *what* and *why* of Acceptance. Now we will move to *how*, *when* and *where*.

Developing consensus and commitment

Events and face-to-face interactions can now be real time in both our physical world as well as in the digital one. We don't recommend beginning in the digital realm unless it is a reinforcement of earlier in-person meetings, although, increasingly, we find ourselves depending on digital communications to simplify meetings or to make global connections possible.

Face-to-face interactions in the physical world remains the most effective and is the number one priority for your engagement with stakeholders. Some examples are presentations, feedback sessions, and informal informational sessions to highly interactive games and events staged as "roadshows".

Our definition of "delay time" means anything that can be accessed by an individual without having to be physically present to benefit. Strategies can include fact sheets, newsletters, and FAQs. All these can be delivered through the company intranet as a website specifically focused on the change initiative.

Delay time strategies do not in any way replace real-time, face-to-face events. Consider the CEO in Chapter Six who presented a powerful case for change as he stood in front of the company's employees. Staff then went immediately into a feedback session with their supervisors, followed by a competition and eventually a visit to the new company headquarters. This entire sequencing was based on people-to-people, high-energy events.

Delay time has an obvious benefit. People can access information and get answers to questions anytime, anywhere through the Internet. Integrity is as essential in delay time as in real-time strategies. Information has to be responsive, transparent and most of all accurate. If your team puts up a FAQ on day one of the Acceptance campaign, and it remains a static document, that's a guaranteed turn off. In fact, there's a lot of negative history with all of us for informational formats that don't reflect feedback and concerns based on current realities.

Setting the stage

Remember the importance of storytelling in the Awareness phase and the examples for how to use stories to draw people into an experience? It's an effective strategy that reaches people at the emotional level, effectively getting past the "noise" of everything else going on in their lives. Now we will need another kind of story, one that first outlines the needs, then selects events and strategies to support those needs.

Here's how this type of strategy worked well with one of our clients:

> When a tax-collection agency needed to revamp its highly entrenched ten-year-old intranet to a feature-rich, dynamic portal, it wanted to cross the river without drowning. The project sponsor believed that managing change was the key to success for this transition. To facilitate this initiative, we called on the agency's internal champions to create interesting activities that would fully engage all stakeholders.
>
> The Change Adoption Plan included a competition, online quizzes, a road show, focus groups, and consultation sessions. The end result was a positively inspired organization looking forward to jumping onto this new, dynamic portal.

Strategies for increasing Acceptance to change

Getting to the task level is as essential in assigning responsibilities as it is in planning any event. Our clients find it helpful to use the engagement plan that follows as the baseline for their decisions, but only after they have developed a story line for how Acceptance can play out.

Stakeholder Engagement Plan

When the need Is ...	Highly impacted stakeholders	Most effective delivery choice	How choice addresses need	Evaluating intervention effectiveness
Gathering opinions and issues to understand concerns and explore potential solutions	High impacted stakeholders that are alike	**Focus Groups**	Stakeholder feels valued and respected when concerns are heard and understood	Survey participants to see if they are satisfied that their concerns have been addressed
Building trust through conscious listening and feedback	Open to all stakeholders who are affected by the change	**Community Meetings**	Different stakeholder groups can understand others' views, creating an environment of openness and trust	Change Support Network evaluates and reports back to the team, using findings to refine Acceptance activities
Developing an interactive participation in new initiative	Open to all stakeholders who are affected by the change	**Road Shows**	Stakeholders get to experience change in an interactive setting that galvanizes and improves readiness	Real-time observation, surveys, and feedback from supervisors and Change Support Network
Exploring changing work patterns in a fun manner	Bonding with peers to help each other with the change	**Games and Challenges**	Stakeholders are inspired to think about the future	Observing level of participation in games and competition
Harvesting reactions and responses to identify roadblocks to change	Open to all stakeholders who are affected by change	**Feedback Channels**	Stakeholders are motivated to express concerns that need attention and action	Change Support Network evaluates and address feedback responsively

When the need Is ...	Highly impacted stakeholders	Most effective delivery choice	How choice addresses need	Evaluating intervention effectiveness
Providing current and pertinent information	For entire organization	**24/7 Out Reach**	Every stakeholder can receive and use information personalized to job function	Team uses it to determine whether employees are getting what they need

This is a not intended as an extensive list. It represents a cross section of possibilities for what proactive delivery systems can accomplish when the goal is to reach the tipping point in favor of Acceptance.

There is no reason, for example, to go to considerable effort to produce a Road Show unless you have evidence it meets the stakeholders' needs, and there is a significant likelihood the event will be successful in meeting expectations. Otherwise you will have a high-profile failure on your hands and find yourself wishing you had heeded this advice. You will be effective only if you choose events and interventions that flow in a way that draws people in, keeps them interested, provides them information as targeted knowledge, and includes some drama or a challenge that builds excitement and camaraderie.

Small missteps are not disasters, especially if you and your team have shown good intention and transparency. For example, a fact sheet is not going to be effective if it is considered a major delivery system, but it won't do major damage as long as the information is accurate and kept updated. An expensive, bells-and-whistles website, on the other hand, if it doesn't meet people's needs, will be a major turnoff for your stakeholders because it won't meet their expectations, and they will note their displeasure or disinterest by not logging on.

The section that follows provides high-level descriptions of the strategies we recommend focused on the "what?" and the "why?" of things we have found to be the most effective implementation strategies.

Focus Groups are powerful in the Acceptance stage

This strategy is valuable early in the process, before you define the rest of your action plan for events and information-delivery channels. An example is the Singapore Ministry of Education's initiative introduced earlier. In this case, the most impacted stakeholders were parents. Inviting a sample group to a session where their opinions and concerns were validated and explored gives the Implementation Team valuable information on how to acquire stakeholder Acceptance.

Strategically, your focus will be on identifying the need and recommending types of participants. Your most important role will be selecting the facilitator, a choice that needs to be carefully made, not just for their skills as a facilitator but as someone who can relate well to the focus group participants.

The facilitator needs to understand that a variety of participants will be involved. They will have various personality types including the expert, the strongly opinionated person, the rambler and the shy participant. A good facilitator knows how to identify and manage these dynamics, levelling the playing field so everyone's opinions are honoured and validated. From this point, the rest of the details can be delegated.

Community Meetings provide a valuable open forum

Community meetings become valuable when they respond to stakeholder concerns. Key elements for success include:

- Making it clear in the invitation that management wants to hear and respond to its stakeholders. There will, of course, be skeptics unless community meetings are already a standard engagement approach in your organization.

- Using your Change Support Network to help market the event and considering having the Change Support Network or line supervisors issue the invitation.

- Understanding the meaning and ramifications of the stakeholder concept before holding such a meeting. Otherwise you can cause the participants to doubt your organization's commitment to this change initiative.

- Listening with an open mind to ideas presented by the participants. They might have insights that can increase efficiency and profits or both.

Road Shows work well if they meet your objectives

Do an Internet search for "road shows learning" or "road shows change initiatives" or a dozen other variations on this theme, and you will come up with everything from car shows to what, in our minds, clearly qualify as workshops, lectures, or brainstorming sessions.

So here's our definition. We see a Road Show as a high-energy, well-executed event in which people learn a new process or acquire essential knowledge through interactive collaboration that results in the empowerment to use a new skill on the job.

Games and Competitions add interest and increase stickiness

Games and competitions all essentially involve the following elements:

- Some form of challenge (interesting quizzes, puzzles, or riddles) that require participants to explore and learn

- A format for participation that allows everyone to jump in and find answers (online or physical) with little time investment

- Some small token prizes for the winners as incentive and to inject an element of fun into the game

Remember that such challenges can be effectively combined with other activities such as a Road Show for even greater impact.

Feedback Channels can strengthen stakeholder commitment

Developing feedback channels can include community meetings, emails, social media, a project website, and participant surveys.

We have described the community meetings earlier, but we need to note here that they can have endless variations, including spontaneous meetings with small groups or forums where a supervisor or member of the support team addresses a particular stakeholder concern and facilitates a discussion.

Emails, text messages, and regular mail have the well-deserved reputation of being "cold" mediums for delivery. They are now used to accept jobs, break off a relationship, or monitor your daily intake of sugar. But email and social media have their place. For example, as a thank-you for attending an event, to acknowledge a feedback message, to notify a specific group of stakeholders that their recommendations have been accepted, or to notify employees who have opted in for notifications about updated project information.

A project website can be valuable when it serves as a legitimate feedback channel. The caveat is that the most dynamic, flash-driven, interactive website does not replace feedback delivered in real time by a real person. A project website has to be vibrant, relevant, punchy, and, above all, have stickiness in order to matter. It's a one-stop location for relevant information relating to the project and can also serve as a feedback channel.

Stakeholders need multiple reasons to visit the project website and be convinced that, once they are there, they will have a meaningful experience. The ability to comment, get feedback, and obtain the latest information is valuable. And when they need to go there because they get clues for a game or a challenge they are involved in, the number of hits on the site is bound to spike.

Digital Communication can be valuable if used well

The menu of communication strategies detailed for the Awareness stage works well at this junction of the cycle.

> It's good to remind yourself on a regular basis that strategies you design and deliver are only as good as the rationale for choosing them.
>
> As the saying goes, you can't make a silk purse out of a sow's ear. But if you could, the silk purse might not be the right accessory for the occasion.

Implementing feedback analysis and moving to Adoption

Here's why this step is so essential. To provide effective learning interventions, you and your team need to analyze the factors that motivate the majority of stakeholders to step into the circle of supporters. This requires compiling the feedback from all the engagement interactions. For transparency and credibility, you need a timeline commitment for providing that analysis to appropriate stakeholders and feedback contributors.

It is critical that the team log what they have learned so it's easily accessible as needed. An ideal situation is the ability to drop these nuggets into knowledge management databases. This requires determining what these nuggets mean to your current change initiative as well as having access to them in the future.

Before you gather feedback, you need to be able to organize it in a way that synthesizes responses, makes meaning of it, and indicates to the reader how it can become a guide for informing this and future projects. Otherwise, the reader might interpret the feedback in a personal way and feed that back to you rather than opinions based on their own experience. Think of it as giving your stakeholders a structure from which they operate and send back targeted, valuable knowledge from their areas of expertise.

In this way, you have a building in which recommendations have a residence and a life.

This process allows your team to become subject-matter experts who transfer knowledge directly to the team that will design the learning experiences in the Adoption phase.

Before analysis begins, you and your team need to ask and answer these questions as you move into Adoption:

- What strengths do your stakeholders bring to Adoption, the period where they learn new skills and attitudes and demonstrate they know how to use them?

- Where are the knowledge and attitudinal gaps?

- How can you best share what you have learned with the Implementation Team that will be instrumental in designing and delivering performance-based learning?

- As you go forward, how can you present it and think about it with each other so that you have tangible scenarios for leading sustainable Adoption strategies?

Where do we go from here?

You might feel like you've finished the job when you've received rave reviews about the road shows, the community meetings, the robust website, and the feedback sessions. Not to disillusion you, but while Acceptance is an essential process, it's not the end result.

At this juncture, the high-energy events are over. Now the continuous work begins in earnest. If Adoption doesn't result in sustainable behavioral change, your hard-earned stakeholder Acceptance will quickly become indifference.

Everything you collect as feedback needs to be evaluated so it can be synthesized and made available to your team as retrievable knowledge to ensure sustainable Adoption. Take a deep breath because that's not all. Conscious communication needs to be folded into the way your organization does business, with the strength and flexibility to survive the waves of change.

We are not suggesting you strive for what you might consider perfection. If you do, you could easily end up wondering who moved your cheese. That can happen when you become fixated on a goal and don't respond to incoming data that signals unexpected change. Instead, you could well be searching in the wrong part of the maze for your dinner.

Like any living organism, your organization has a life of its own. We humans are not only advanced enough to change the world but unpredictable enough in our emotional landscape to surprise others and occasionally even ourselves. Consider again that while you have the strategic telescopic view for adapting to change, staff and other stakeholders are hunkered over their microscopes trying to figure out how change will impact them individually. It's not that one view is right and the other is wrong. Instead, the different views need to link conscious communication to authentic feedback.

This is new territory for everyone. The commitment-based approach is the best choice if you want stakeholders to accept change and commit to adoption. The world is too volatile and complex to operate any other way. It starts with believing in yourself, keeping your team inspired, and empowering your stakeholders to see the benefit of being fully engaged in the learning mode so they can act on and play their role as they ride the waves of change.

That brings us to Adoption, the subject of our last implementation chapter but not, by any stretch of the imagination, the end of the story.

And by the way, it would be a great idea to invite your team to a dinner where you don't talk shop. Instead, enjoy each other's company, applaud yourselves for what you have achieved, and anticipate success as you join the stakeholders in increasing your own knowledge and change-readiness skills.

You didn't think this process was just for everyone else, did you? Your authentic, effective leadership depends on staying ahead of the pack with your own commitment regime. It's about walking the talk.

CHAPTER EIGHT
Facilitating Adoption

Knowledge is not the power. The ability to act on Knowledge is Power.
— Michael Schrage, co-director, MIT's Media Lab

In This Chapter

You will discover why the process of Adoption is the foundation for your change initiative. More importantly, we will demonstrate how you can grow into an effective leader who understands what it takes to create a culture of high performers. You will learn the dance of embracing accountability as you delegate and then effectively monitor the processes you are using. Your role will be to influence, mentor, and persuade while always leading from the front.

A key element of Adoption is the enthusiastic embrace of this concept. Adoption is not the final step in any change initiative. Instead, it is the bridge that enables people to become sustainable players in the twenty-first century Knowledge Economy. While the Awareness and Acceptance phases are redefined and reshaped for each new change initiative, Adoption is the ongoing process in which your organization commits to people development as an essential business practice. This message flows throughout this chapter. Awareness and Acceptance sell the initiative to stakeholders. Adoption hands the power to individual employees who see how they are part of the solution, not part of the problem.

Defining Adoption

In the near term, Adoption is the process by which your people acquire new skills specific to a change initiative. They will begin the Adoption journey, accepting and acting on their role in making organizational change successful. While the training and development department, with your team's input, will design, deliver, and administer the selected learning strategies for change initiatives, your team must take ownership. Otherwise, you've planned an elaborate dinner party, but only half the invited guests show up, and the ones who do are busy texting their friends or trying to slip out of the room unnoticed.

Long term, Adoption must become a core value within your organization. To ensure success, your Change Facilitation Team will want to continuously monitor the effectiveness of learning interventions by tracking how, when, and where your stakeholders learn effectively. This enables your people-development team to make adjustments for different styles of learning, resulting in increased performance and buy-in. But it won't help if your stakeholders are learning outdated concepts and skills that haven't kept pace with global change and changes inside your organization.

What does Adoption mean for leaders like you?

We want to get this out of the way at the top of the chapter so you are clear about your pivotal role in this process. You need to be strategically accountable for increased performance at all levels of this initiative and for all stakeholders. This accountability is a logical extension of a role you have already assumed. But it's not yet as familiar to you as other aspects of the Adaptive Path Framework.

Here's where bringing a manager from training and development into the process early in the change cycle is going to pay huge dividends. By having that manager participate in and provide input into the Awareness and Acceptance stages, you arrive at Adoption knowing more about how training and development function in your organization.

This way the training manager now understands the change initiative goals through personal experience with the Implementation and Change Support Teams throughout the Awareness and Acceptance cycles. Obviously, this is highly preferable to planning meetings for this stage where you each find yourself operating in parallel universes in which neither of you understands the other's worldview or frame of reference. Armed with the language of the training/learning domain, using your expanding managerial skills and empowered by the assistance of your Change Support Network, you will gain your footing effectively.

It is essential that all stakeholders understand how this new way of learning is going to benefit them. Put on your marketing hat because you are going to be selling again.

Criteria for building sustainable performance bridges

Everyone – from the CEO to line staff – needs to commit to and be involved with new skills and expanded mind-sets to make change initiatives successful. As we continue to emphasize, leaders need to commit to their own learning as the most effective way to model the vision for stakeholders. This means that the delivery systems for learning and performance support are not the strategic domain of human resources, training and development, or any other department, but are actively led by senior management. Instructional-design teams drive development, but not strategy. Otherwise, stakeholders are getting the microscopic and not the telescopic view for how their learning is designed.

As opposed to the usual scenario in which management makes a decision and the training department signs, seals, and delivers in the usual lockstep style, key delivery systems for Adoption need to be integrated into the entire implementation cycle. If you have successfully led the Awareness and Acceptance cycles, essential stakeholder groups in the organization will already have participated in delivery systems that will now be familiar to them in the Adoption phase. The addition of online learning to delivery choices then becomes a natural extension of the conscious communication principles stakeholders have been experiencing throughout the implementation cycle.

Getting Help from Experts
It's time to bring everyone's expertise into the mix.
Include marketing, training, and organizational development

Why Adoption is critical and your role essential

For a long list of reasons, Adoption is not usually included in most frameworks for change initiatives. We suspect you might feel some resistance to the idea that involvement in learning initiatives should be added to your already full plate. If you are dragging around that old mind-set, it's time to let it go. As we will demonstrate, nothing could be further from the truth.

Think of it this way: would you rather have accountability for ensuring Adoption that provides a difference in the bottom line? Or do you prefer to stand by watching a carefully orchestrated change initiative fail to make it to the winner's circle?

When executives consider delivering performance-based training, they are likely to think about high-end Learning Management Systems that track each employee's progress and identify knowledge gaps. There is definitely value in that functionality. What it doesn't track is the individually specific and illusively emotional landscape of each of your stakeholders. And as we all know by now, that human element, while absolutely essential, is likely to be unpredictable.

Learning strategies that result in increased performance doesn't have to be a big budget item. As we have seen in the last two chapters, simple interventions can be remarkably effective. This chapter will help you understand your role and how you will need to empower those who will be directly involved in designing and sometimes delivering the Learning Action Plan.

The need for training, knowledge transfer, and access to concise information on demand is not limited to your employees. Each of your external stakeholder groups might need some type of intervention if the change initiative has created new knowledge or updated information. A complicated initiative could have a dozen or more stakeholder groups with varying levels of impact and profiles that determine the style and type of follow-up or intervention.

Strategies could also be as simple as a meeting for your external partners where you test the water to determine if they are in need of information, clarification, or just a pep talk, and then systematically check in with all key partners to make certain your change initiative is working well on their side.

These external partners might also appreciate seeing progress reports and the corporate newsletter or website relating to the initiative. However, like you, external partners have a full plate with their own organizations so remind yourself to give them only the level of interaction and information they need to support your initiative. That will vary from partner to partner. At one end of the spectrum is an executive who needs more frequent contact because he has a difficult boss, and at the other end of that spectrum is the partner who lets you know she will contact you if she needs anything.

Stakeholders and stockholders value your involvement

Traditionally, senior management and training-development departments have played a protracted game of table tennis. For obvious reasons, senior management wants to see a return-on-investment for its training budgets. Training people return the ball and point out examples that include the intangible nature of leadership development and the expense of quantifying the effectiveness of workplace performance. From there the volley goes back and forth in a frustrating zero-to-zero game.

And so it went until a researcher decided to use an entirely different, remarkably simple strategy that found a direct correlation between an organization's commitment to training and stock market performance!

The research done by Laurie Bassi, the CEO of McBassi & Company and a Ph.D. in economics from Princeton University, found that firms spending more on training are likely to outperform other companies. When she profiled firms, Bassi discovered that those making the largest per capita investments in training subsequently returned 16.3 percent per year compared to 10.7 percent for the S&P 500 index. And it seems logical that this research can be used to draw a more general correlation that companies that put people first, in a broad sense, strengthen their bottom line.

This might come as a surprise, but your stakeholders see training as a valuable benefit. It can align them with your strategic mission and result in increased loyalty to the organization. Don Clark, an instructional designer and respected thought leader, believes this might explain some of the surge in leadership training. The job market is slowly but surely tightening. Even finding good unskilled labor is getting slightly more difficult. And these workers are asking for training that will help them to advance.

Global challenges in developing high performers

While different challenges exist in developing and developed countries, no country has consistently produced people who perform at their maximum effectiveness. It's possible to make technology perform seamlessly, but humans obviously don't operate that way. This is evidenced dramatically across the Asian Pacific region.

Even though countries such as Singapore, Japan, and Korea have achieved universal education, knowledge and performance gaps remain.

This is true in the Western Hemisphere as well. These problems, of course, are complicated dramatically by the necessity of having a workforce able to shift both skill-sets and mind-sets as they find themselves in the vortex of unprecedented change. Singapore made its rapid transformation from a cluster of Malay fishing villages to a world power in mere decades.

People performance in the 21st century

Here's a high-level look at the ways in which the Knowledge Economy changes the criteria for how the realities of the twenty-first century are changing the way we work and ultimately the way we demonstrate high-level competency:

- A knowledge-based economy relies primarily on the use of ideas as opposed to physical abilities and the application of technology.

- In such an economy, most businesses don't transform raw materials or exploit cheap labor. Instead, knowledge is developed and applied in new ways.

- Product cycles are shorter and the need for innovation greater. Trade is expanding worldwide, increasing competitive demands on producers.

- The global Knowledge Economy is transforming the demands of the labor market in economies throughout the world.

- It is also placing new demands on citizens, who need more skills and knowledge to be able to function in their day-to-day lives.

- Equipping people to deal with these demands requires a new model of education and training to one of lifelong learning.

- A lifelong-learning framework encompasses learning throughout the life cycle, from early childhood to retirement.

- It includes formal learning (schools, training institutions, universities), non-formal learning (on-the-job and in-house training), and informal education such as skills learned from family members or people in the community.

- It allows people to access learning opportunities, as they need them rather than because they have reached a certain age.

- Lifelong learning is crucial to preparing staff to compete in the global economy. It starts by encouraging employees to be contributing members of their communities.

That was a full food-for-thought meal. And speaking of food, you might want to take a break here, note a few questions you still have, then come back to this chapter after you have time to incubate the essential nature of Adoption principles.

How did you learn to be a manager?

While our description won't fit your profile precisely, we are guessing it goes something like this: you came out of college with an undergraduate degree in business, information technology, accounting, or some other specialist area that found you first participating in and then leading projects. Along the way, you might have picked up a project management certification, attended conferences with gurus in your field, and taken classes for honing leadership skills. In addition to project management skills, you likely have delegating responsibility to others and taking the accountability part of your job down to a science. If not, you wouldn't have made it to your current position. Are we on track so far?

You found some elements of training and development effective, but for the most part, you learned on the job, watching others, getting into your "groove," discovering your strengths, and compensating for your soft skills such as communication. You might have found communicating effectively with your superiors, peers, and the employees who reported directly or indirectly to you more frustrating, a skill that had a steep learning curve.

At this point, we recommend you acknowledge accountability for all aspects of your change initiatives including Adoption. You might be thinking that we have you mixed up with someone else. The truth is, we don't, so bear with us while we unfold the rest of this stage of the Adaptive Path. As we get more specific about delivery systems for people development, the conceptual ideas we have outlined early in this chapter will begin to come into focus.

If you keep in mind that you are always leading from the front, you will begin to identify the concepts you are acquiring here as being not only foundational to your stakeholders, but essential for your own skill building.

One of the key challenges for senior managers is that you ideally have experience with many things while you are master of none. Most of what you do is delegate and strive to make others accountable. It's a complex job. We have found that, with the right knowledge tools and support, our clients step up to the challenge, sometimes surprising themselves. Watching those "aha" moments unfold are gratifying, particularly because we are also learning about ourselves as we mentor others.

Adults have well-defined learning criteria in common

While others have tried to arrive at their personal versions of adult-learning theory, no one touches Malcolm Knowles, the pioneer in that field. We believe he got it right. His principles include:

- **Learners have a need to learn.**
  Facilitators offer new possibilities, clarify learner needs, and then diagnose gaps between current performance and optimal outcomes.

- **The learning environment is important.**
  It is characterized by physical comfort; mutual respect, trust, and helpfulness; freedom of expression; and acceptance of differences.

- **Learners take ownership of their learning experience.**
  Facilitators involve the students in a mutual process of formulating learning.

- **The learners participate actively in the learning process.**
  There are infinite ways to involve adult learners, including giving them choices.

- **The learning process makes use of learner experience.**
  Facilitators need to gear the presentation of their own resources to the levels of experience of the learners, making learning more relevant and integrated.

- **The learners have a sense of progress toward their goals**
  Facilitators need to make the experience a process of reaching learner goals.

- **Learners and facilitators collaborate in a process of evaluation.**
  This mirrors the philosophy of honoring your employees as adults.

Essential Adoption elements

You have discovered how the Adaptive Path Framework works and developed an understanding for the critical and complex role of stakeholders. Now it's game time! Here are some high-level points to keep in mind as you interact with stakeholders up and down the chain.

- The end game is not about learning, although that is essential. It is about performing with enthusiasm and competence.

- After an intervention, analyze what worked and what didn't. If this seems like too much work, consider the hole you will need to climb out of as well as the possibility of never reclaiming lost momentum and credibility.

- Acknowledge that the process of managing an ongoing, effective performance-based learning culture is more complicated in Adoption than in Acceptance. In that stage, the Adaptive Path focuses on specific real-time events and delay-time strategies for keeping people informed and updated about the change initiative.

Performance Learning Plan

Plan to review the Performance Learning Plan (refer to the Resources) so you have a strategic grasp of the steps your training and development people will be using to create delivery systems based on our learning model.

The chart that follows represents a foundational element of our Adaptive Path Framework. Leading performance support experts also validate what we have found through our client engagements.

Figure 8 - KDi's Learning Model for Sustainable Performance

Using our learning model during the design, development, and delivery of learning experiences strengthens learning and performance-support interventions.

Because people do not learn new skills and acquire expertise passively, we recommend:

- Coaching, followed by training
- Simulations of real-world situations so people can safely practice
- Informal mentoring in the workplace
- Performance support available at the moment of need

It is exciting to discover that our Awareness, Acceptance, and Adoption cycle is exactly the way people not only change mind-sets but learn. It is ultimately the way everyone takes charge of their learning. We share the strong belief that when any kind of learning intervention falls short, as they often do, it is because organizations failed to adopt practices that mirror what we all need in order to reach the point of self-discovery as sustainable Adoption.

How our Adoption framework is unique

First and foremost, it is based on a Stakeholder Analysis that utilizes our powerful Change Support Network. Refresh and check your findings from earlier in the Adaptive Path Framework. Survey your employees again to ask what's working and what's not, and then share the results with links to relevant Performance Support topics. Remind employees how to access Performance Support when they have an issue. Then use the analytics to show the most frequent topics that employees have accessed.

A sustainable performance strategy can be as informal as a supervisor coaching an employee on a new piece of equipment or as sophisticated as databases delivered to mobile devices that result in improved people performance. Such a strategy can take many forms, but those forms have common characteristics, including alignment with performance needs.

While learning in a self-paced digital environment needs to be considered for its multiple benefits, such learning must be grounded in real-time communication, in person and online. Delivery systems need to be selected based on a core principle – the foundation of what we believe – that people and the quality of authentic communications are more important than anything else.

None of the delivery systems we are proposing in this action plan will be useful as a single response to a pivotal learning/attitude-shifting challenge. Like the rest of the Adaptive Path, successful Adoption is about a flow of experiences that results in benefits all stakeholders can immediately use, with options for deepening and expanding the learning experience over time. Selecting a varied menu of delivery systems will provide opportunities for different styles of learning so that people will experience what is natural for them. From that more psychologically secure position, they will be able to practice expanding to modalities that are not part of their natural strengths.

Everyone, from the CEO to line staff, need to commit to and be involved in learning new skills and expanding mind-sets in order to make change initiatives successful.

Senior management must lead Adoption

This means that the delivery systems for learning and performance support are not the domain of the human resources, organizational development or the training functions, but are strategically led by senior managers who should have ultimate accountability for optimal Adoption effectiveness. Instructional design teams drive development but not strategy. Otherwise, learners will get a view from the microscope and not the telescope.

As opposed to the standard scenario in which management makes a decision and training is initiated in the usual lock-step style, key delivery systems for Adoption need to be integrated into the entire implementation cycle.

Here's how our learning model helped one of our clients:

> A Singapore-based company purchased Unitrust management software with a backend processing database for fund managers at more than twenty fund houses. The goal was to significantly enhance the company's operational capability by streamlining the existing workflow and sharing large amounts of information currently unavailable to the right people.
>
> But buying the expensive system didn't solve the problem. When the company implemented the new system, it captured information but did not improve the workflow, making the information useless to the frustrated employees because the processes were not redesigned to address daily work scenarios that needed improvement.
>
> After analyzing the client's situation, we created enhanced work scenarios and then trained operators and middle management while we coached upper management so its members were all aware of and involved in the solution. Using our learning-model criteria, we initiated relevant learning strategies.
>
> We also delivered sparse but essential training. Rather than putting employees through hours of time-consuming feature-based training or online learning, we provided them a quick introduction to the most important new features. Then we gave the business scenarios, illustrating new and productive ways to work

individually and in teams. Most importantly, we focused training efforts on showing the employees how to find answers when they were stuck or confused.

These learning interventions empowered knowledge transfer by supporting performance in the Microsoft applications to make sure employees were able to solve their own issues in two clicks and ten seconds.

This follows our philosophy that embedded performance support must be both context sensitive and provide "just enough" support to get employees back to work quickly.

It's not possible to achieve 100% stakeholder Adoption,
but being on the Adaptive Path with a dynamic map to guide you is definitely preferable to wandering in the wilderness.

Adoption as sustainable performance

After you have successfully lead the Awareness and Acceptance cycles, everyone in the organization will have participated in delivery systems that will now be familiar to them in the Adoption phase. The addition of online training and performance support to delivery choices then becomes a natural extension of the interactive communication principles people have been experiencing throughout the implementation cycle.

While the Performance Learning Plan in the Resources section is essential to the people who develop learning interventions, we take an approach that we believe you will find more relevant from a strategic perspective. Familiarize yourself with the Adoption plan so you can have informed conversations with the training and development department.

Dr. Conrad Gottfredson and Bob Mosher of Ontuitive believe we are now in the world of "knowledge activation," which includes concepts and task mastery evidenced with on-the-job competence as continuous improvement.

They have identified five moments of need:

- Learning for the first time.
- Learning more.
- Applying what one has learned.
- Figuring out what to do when something goes wrong.
- Figuring out what to do when something changes.

We think Gottfredson and Mosher have it figured out. Beyond all the learning theories and complexities for designing learning, these "moments of need" can effectively guide us to those points where we need to learn more. We can also move to strategies that deliver those "moments of need" to individuals and groups in the ways they learn best.

Here's an example of research about the brain that was applied to performance support. It's essential for online performance support to give a complete answer without moving to a new page or screen. That's because the mind shifts its thinking when the eyes have to shift.

Did you ever walk into a room with some purpose in mind, only to forget why you were there? Here's good news. It turns out doors are to blame for memory lapses. Psychologists at the University of Notre Dame have discovered that passing through a doorway triggers what's known as "an event boundary" in the mind, separating one set of thoughts and memories from the next. Your brain files away the thought you had in the previous room and prepares a blank page in your brain for the new locale.

We recommend using the term "people developers" to describe the job functions of training, human resources, and OD functions.

Creating positive relationships with people developers

Your team, and especially your Change Support Network are the subject-matter experts. You have been collaborating using a strategic view of the change process while you are going operational. You know what has worked, and through continuing needs analysis, you understand what your stakeholders know as well as where the knowledge/motivation gaps exist. Now it's time to collaborate with training departments.

What follows are some basic guidelines as you build experience.

- Demonstrate a well-defined position where you are in charge of learning interventions because you are accountable while the training and development departments have the responsibility. Make this clear upfront. You don't want the training department telling you what it needs instead of working in collaboration with you.

- Review and modify the Needs Analysis described in Chapter Five so it addresses what you have learned from stakeholders in the implementation stages.

- As the development of interventions progresses, be prepared to mediate between IT and the training department if your plans involve online learning and performance support. Your bottom-line mantra is this. Training needs to drive technology, or any delivery system for that matter, and not the reverse.

Fact-finding with those who lead people development

Questions like the ones below will establish you as the strategic leader of the Adoption process:

- You have had a chance to work on the Awareness and Acceptance phases for this change initiative. How do you think what you learned will help with implementing the Adoption stage?

- What do you consider some successful training interventions you have been responsible for or you have experienced and benefited from as a learner?

- What strategies have you found that work best in motivating learners to take on new learning challenges?

- How can we reduce resistance to learning new skills? Note: Knowledge and learning are the keys to Adoption particularly when it involves new skill sets that can create uncertainties and require new learning.

- What kind of strategies can we use that take advantage of people's learning differences? How, for example, should learning be designed for the sales team as opposed to administrative assistants?

Take note: essential to remember

Learning in a self-paced digital environment needs to be considered for its multiple benefits, but foundational learning must be grounded in real-time communication, in person and online. Delivery system needs should be selected based on the core principle that people and the quality of authentic communications are the foundation of the change initiative and more important than anything else. None of the delivery systems in the action plan we have detailed in Resources will be useful as a single response to a pivotal learning/attitude-shifting challenge.

Successful Adoption is about a flow of experiences
resulting in benefits all stakeholders can immediately use,
with options for deepening and expanding
the learning experience over time.

Leaders must be involved in their own cycle of learning

You and your team need to initiate your own development training so your leadership becomes increasingly fluid, scenario-based, and thoughtfully adaptive. All senior managers need to have a high-level understanding of the most effective delivery system for sustainable learning and performance support. We advise them to facilitate or at least attend some face-to-face sessions described in the Performance Learning Plan, found in the Resources section so they have a tangible understanding of stakeholder groups' successes as well as challenges in adapting to unfamiliar and possibly more complex work processes.

Representatives from the Implementation Team, especially the Change Support Network, should arrange with training departments to take some of the online learning modules their employees are taking. This gives the Change Support Network experiential understanding and talking points with groups of stakeholders. Can you imagine how relieved a group of logistics employees, with no experience in online learning, would feel when someone in the Change

Support Network sits with them over coffee and talks about the challenges she had with learning online and how she found it effective once she became familiar with learning in a different environment?

The Implementation Team needs to encourage developers to adapt a diverse menu of delivery strategies. This will provide opportunities for people with a variety of learning and operational styles to experience what is natural for them. From that more psychologically secure position, they will be able to practice expanding to modalities that are not their natural strengths.

Recommendations for your active role in Adoption

- **Stay strategic**
  In this part of the cycle, we have taken a different tactic than in the chapters on Awareness and Acceptance. That's because your role in the earlier stages is more direct than in Adoption. That doesn't mean it's less important. In many ways, the opposite is true. You will always turn the Adoption role over to another group with expertise in how people learn and how to design and deliver that learning.

  The Performance Learning Plan is provided so you can have meaningful conversations with human resources and training managers. You will want to return to this chapter frequently so you can evaluate whether the programs they are designing and delivering to stakeholders meet the immediate needs of the current change initiative and build toward an organizational culture focused on learning as a proactive response to rapid, often unexpected, change.

- **Sell benefits**
  Review Chapter Six with its focus on storytelling as stickiness. Take a marketing manager to lunch and pick his brain for ideas on how to sell the benefits of learning.

- **Think big, start small**
  This applies particularly to investments in technology. Stories of massive investments in technology – where leaders had no idea how those systems would be used – are legend. Two decades ago, everyone wanted to jump on the technology bandwagon, an apparent answer to all our training challenges. Working with the developers you can design a plan that will

maximize technology by effectively exploiting its strengths. Under no circumstances should you turn your learning initiatives over to a machine.

- **Be tangible**
  Recommend specific strategies to people developers.

- **Lead in each new stage of the Adaptive Path cycle**
  Use face-to-face interventions, starting with the Awareness phase, moving on to Acceptance, and then to Adoption.

- **Implement performance support**
  Use a spectrum of strategies, but focus them on online access for getting help when and where it's needed.

- **Deliver new processes as interactive training**
  These processes should be face-to-face, online or a combination.

- **Consider that one strategy works in one part of a cycle but may not in another**
  For example, rather than Road Shows, which we have found extremely effective for ensuring Acceptance, consider that in the Adoption phase, facilitating a series of seminars before the kick-off of new learning can be more effective than a Road Show.

- **Encourage informal learning using the Performance Learning Plan**
  Remind yourself that while it can't be wrapped in a bow and delivered, informal learning is happening all the time from the boardroom to the lunchroom.

  Some of that learning might be less than optimal, but it should be encouraged: if people have more integrated support for their learning process, the questions they ask and the responses they get will be higher quality.

- **Offer incentives and rewards**
  There is ongoing debate as to whether incentives should be offered to people who complete training or demonstrate excellence through testing or performance.

While in an ideal world, each person would feel the reward internally and not need an incentive, there are situations where a bit of healthy competition can be a good motivator.

You will be the best judge of what works in your organizational culture. If rewards are the only motivator, increased performance won't be sustainable. If, for example, your organization has spent time and money on an innovative learning approach in response to a major change, a competition or reward for demonstrating excellence could be just what the doctor ordered.

Where do we go from here?

From here, it's about navigating continuous change. Without that full-out commitment to excellence for you and your organization, you will find yourself in a cycle in which every change initiative is a blank page.

With a commitment to leading from the front, you sign on for the long term. This means that ongoing reflection is essential for you and your team. It provides a pause to consider what worked well, what was a waste of time, or, worst case scenario, what almost took your project under. Taking what you have learned into the future is essential for leading planned change.

Before you begin the final section, we strongly suggest you take the time for the reflective exercise and use it with your team. When you consciously and proactively take on change, you are changed forever.

Reflecting on Implementing Change

A Team Reflection to Engage Innovative Thinking

Set the Stage

Read Nancy's story about the tornado and how it defines change (refer to page 1 of the book)

Lead your team in considering these questions

- What does change now look and feel like to you?
- How do others in the organization now perceive change?
- What evidence do you have that your view of how others have changed is valid?
- What does it tell you about work you still need to do?

Who has to see all these views clearly?

(Facilitator walks around the room and hold a mirror in front of each person). Nancy's experience with the mirror exercise is that it always elicits laughter and a sense of camaraderie since we are all in this together.

And isn't it fortunate we aren't in it alone?

Navigate Change

Leadership Role

Actualizing the future
Leading from the front

Navigating Continuous Change

What leaders need to know

Why Navigating Continuous Change Is Essential

- Sustainability is only possible when an organization truly adopts the concept of continuous change.

- It starts with acknowledgement that a middle path for incremental change gives tangibility to the vision we all aspire to.

- We hold both the vision and commitment while acknowledging that a static vision is never realized because it is, of necessity, a moving target.

What It Takes to Navigate Continuous Change

- Innovation as sustainable change is only possible when we "own" it.

- Leading from the front requires resilience, humility and full-on commitment.

- Reflection with others as well as self-reflection is essential for navigating continuous change.

CHAPTER NINE
Actualizing the Future

Change is a future state with its roots in the present.
Dr. Nancy Harkrider, Partner, KDi

In This Chapter

To give context to this subject, we will introduce you to some predictions from futurists, but keep in mind that trends are simply educated projections based on what we already know.

While change is about moving to a future time, leading change is about supporting ourselves and our stakeholders so that decisions made today can have a positive influence on how we deal with future change.

We will introduce you to scenario planning, a strategy that empowers you and your team to spend time in a mental space distinctly different from your day-to-day work life. If done well, it will allow you to manage unexpected change because you have been rehearsing it by using the Adaptive Path to implement planned initiatives.

Values at the heart of our Adaptive Path Framework

- **Changes begin with organizational structure**
  Organizations based on agility, as opposed to the traditional hierarchical culture, are a positive migration because it allows more flexible response to change. And it follows that this more fluid structure increases the need for leading from the front.

- **People are the drivers of change**
  Achieving Awareness, Acceptance, and ultimately Adoption is only possible through winning the hearts and minds of stakeholders.

Both analytical and creative thinking skills need to be supported at every level or your organization.

- **People communicate and learn in two worlds**
  The digital world has given us options for maximizing that 24/7 world. People collaborating in the face-to-face world must balance that digital world. It's not about either/or but about identifying the best communication mode for maximum results. Over time, attention to where communication thrives will become a sustainable organizational strength.

Plan for the worst while engaging with change in the present

Our ability to lead in crisis mode demands that we use times of relative stability to sharpen our leadership skills and apply lessons learned from following the Adaptive Path. This allows us to navigate unplanned change that is fast moving, unpredictable, and sometimes catastrophic.

It's no accident that our model is well positioned to deal effectively with whatever the future tosses our way by guiding the process of building our "change muscles" on a day-by-day, moment-by-moment basis.

The call you dread and the reality that day will come

We now know that the most difficult trends to grasp are the ones that are of crisis proportion. The tidal waves that periodically devastate the planet have been significantly worse in areas where leaders didn't prepare for an event they failed to anticipate. This reality increases the urgency for implementing change initiatives we do control so we have some baselines for operating effectively in a crisis.

Our clients validate the benefit of preparation for the unexpected
by accomplishing cultural change that develops flexible leaders and takes advantage of a strong support network.

Consider how much worse the hurricane that hit New York in late 2012 could have been had governments not prepared themselves to deal with other kinds of emergencies. Reeling from the trauma of 9/11, the city's leaders identified what they needed to improve and then acted on it. And while their response to the hurricane was less than optimal, we can bet they began immediately taking a strategic look at what they learned so they will be better prepared for the next major emergency. It is a reality that we live in a world in which major disruptive events are not an "if" but a "when."

What the trending gurus are saying

In their book *Foresight 2020*, Jack Uldrich and Simon Anderson identified some broad trends worth considering:

- Automation and process improvements will continue to be a major focus of activity in many companies.

- The search for competitive advantage will increasingly focus on improving the productivity and performance of knowledge workers. This is validated in our work with clients who are acting on their own sustainable commitment to Adoption.

- Specialization will be a defining trend at the organizational level and below. Industries will polarize in response to commoditization. Processes will be outsourced to locations where they are done best. Products and services will become more personalized.

- Collaboration inside and outside companies will widen and deepen as internal teams work across time zones and functions, as customers demand ever more of companies, and as companies demand ever more of suppliers. Relationship skills will be at a premium.

- Technology will help knowledge workers perform better, thanks to new collaboration and communications tools; new ways to store, filter, and retrieve unstructured data; and decision-support tools that expand and enhance knowledge workers' abilities.

- Organizations will become flatter and less hierarchical. Employees will be given greater decision-making autonomy and will participate more actively in corporate planning. Leaders need to be in place at all levels of the Knowledge Economy- focused organizations.

Ernst and Young identify the six trends they believe will redefine business success, and we agree that these trends are important to internalize and then act on.

- "The increasing political and economic dominance of emerging markets will cause global companies to rethink and customize their corporate strategies.

- Climate change will remain high on the agenda as companies seek to explore resource efficiency to improve their bottom line and drive competitive advantage.

- The financial landscape will look vastly different as increasing regulation and government intervention drive restructuring and new business models.

- Governments will play an increasingly prominent role in the private sector as demand for greater regulation and increasing fiscal pressures dominate the agenda.

- Emerging-market innovations and a focus on instant communication anytime, anywhere will drive technology in its next evolution.

- Leaders will need to address the needs and aspirations of an increasingly diverse twenty-first century workforce. "

Pause for a moment and think about how each of these trends might play out in your organization.

Consider how other trends are impacting your organization

Knoll Research offers five future trends to round out this overview. The first two trends have been around for more than a quarter of a century:

- The continuing distribution of organizations in which increasing numbers of employees work remotely or in combination with face-to-face environments

- The availability of enabling technologies and social-collaboration tools in an environment that mirrors the speed of change

The last three trends focus on people issues. There are no surprises here:

- The coming shortage of knowledge workers, a challenge we are addressing with our clients through a focus on adopting strategies that bring performance support to center stage

- The demand for more work flexibility

- Pressure for more sustainable organizations and work styles

A different kind of planning for a chaotic world

The Road Trip from Hell : Consider these situations:

You are the driver on a several-day road trip. A competent driver in city traffic, you have never driven on highways. What do you know already? What skills do you need, and how will you learn them without actually getting on the highway and risking an accident?

Now let's complicate this story line. Imagine you have never driven. But after you are on the road, there is an emergency, and you have to take the wheel for an extremely exhausting road trip across uncharted territory that includes a dangerous mountain range with deep valleys that often flood.

In the first scenario, you are in some ways qualified to be the driver, but you would certainly want to practice highway driving for short periods, building up slowly to road-warrior competence.

The second scenario involves dangers that might end in disaster. This is clearly an unplanned situation of crisis proportions because you are out on the road, without skills, without provisions, without a vehicle that offers a reasonable chance of getting you through a frightening, possibly fatal adventure.

If anything is certain, it is that change is certain.
The world we are planning for today will not exist in this form tomorrow.
– Phillip B. Crosby, businessman and author

This is the essence of the Adaptive Path in which you acquire skills through leadership in planned-change initiatives

Now consider how the first driving scenario can give you basic road-driving skills that will be enormously helpful when you are once again in the driver's seat racing at top speed into totally uncharted territory.

As we have demonstrated with the road-trip examples, scenarios aren't complicated to create if you base them on the following steps:

- Identify what could be a future disaster for your organization.
- Confirm your team accepts or is at least open to participating.
- Block the time needed away from distractions.
- Use a compelling story to give vitality to a problem.
- Work with a skilled facilitator.

That's the organizing part. The complicated side is what you do with the knowledge you have gained in your scenario-planning sessions. That's where the commitment from you and your team in collaboration with a facilitator come into play. Unless you use these scenarios to improve leadership skills and change processes starting in the present, they won't help with your change efforts in normal situations. They definitely won't help when all hell breaks loose and normal becomes chaos.

Scenarios deal with two worlds: the world of facts and the world of perceptions. They explore for facts but they aim at perceptions inside the heads of decision-makers. Their purpose is to gather and transform information of strategic significance into fresh perceptions.

Harvard Business Review

A look at the basics of scenario planning

Scenario planning is a structured approach to visualizing how alternative futures might happen. It can be an equally powerful strategy in small and large organizations. Unlike the future trends earlier in this chapter, they are not predictions or forecasts. Instead, they are more like story lines that explain how current trends and developments could logically play out, resulting in the emergence of a particular future landscape. On the other hand, if the trends evolve in a somewhat different way, then a different strategy will probably emerge.

Scenarios are not about *how to* but about the *why* process based on strategic considerations. Scenarios don't have to be complicated, but they do need to be structured. It won't make a difference unless you know why you are going through the process and how the process will be used. And it's not accomplished in an afternoon. At least a full day at a time is required, away from your office, and with digital devices off, perhaps even checking them at the door.

One thing we can tell you for certain: Scenario planning works because it contains elements of theater. Instead of being an observer, however, you and your team are the actors for a script you have created. You might want to hire an actor to join you for the first session to help you warm up to the idea. There's no reason why serious work can't also be enjoyable!

Once you and your team get some experience with scenario planning, it gets much more fluid, and you will begin to discover how to include other stakeholders up and down the chain. A casual approach is worse than useless because it leaves everyone involved with a negative impression. These four questions will become your signposts on the journey:

- What if?
- What then?
- What can we do now?
- How does this help us prepare for unplanned change?

Remember, this is only an overview of scenario planning as a powerful strategy. It's offered for consideration as you navigate continuous change.

You will know you are on the right track when someone on your team asks *What does that tell us about our current challenge?"*

Where do we go from here?

We believe that well-executed preparation will be a clear advantage for you and your team as you deal with change in the next ten minutes as well as change in the next ten years. It could provide the difference in disaster and success when that heart-stopping road trip is over and things return to "normal."

As much we would like to think otherwise, the part of our brain that is on automatic pilot is still functioning in the twentieth century and desperately fighting against the change our frontal lobe knows is necessary. The only way we can override that nonverbal part of our brain is to build strong, positive leadership experiences in the "new normal" so your authentic leadership is not only natural but also fluid.

While crises are speeding up, so is innovation, particularly if you seize the opportunity to lead from the front, the subject of our last chapter.

CHAPTER TEN
Leading from the Front

It's not the strongest that survive, nor the most intelligent
but the most adaptable to change.
– Charles Darwin, English naturalist

In This Chapter

Trends in leadership development are changing quickly. We're not referring to the concept of leadership itself, but to the act of developing internally as you mentor leadership abilities in others. This shift will offer significant opportunity to demonstrate leading from the front when you take on the challenges of consciously embracing change. In that environment, you and your team can be successful as you adapt to change while staying true to your essential selves. It's a balance between building internal strength and having meaningful relationships with others.

You need to wear multiple hats in your leadership roles. Your superiors and colleagues might view those hats differently, and staff may have yet another image of your headgear. Of course, when you look in the mirror, your internal lens sees those hats in yet a different way. In the midst of managing multiple roles, it's essential that you, as a leader, have a healthy self-awareness, monitoring yourself routinely to make certain you are being true to yourself.

In this chapter, we provide some strategies and recommendations for leading from the front. That leadership is dependent on your being able to stay grounded in the present without ever losing sight of the telescopic view into the future.

This is our core value, and one we share with passion.

Leading from the front begins here

John Kotter, a professor at the Harvard Business School, has created an eight-step model of change that has stood the test of time. Those steps include:

- Establishing a sense of urgency
- Creating the guiding coalition
- Developing a change vision
- Communicating the vision for buy-in
- Generating short term wins
- Never letting up
- Incorporating change into the culture

This is a high-level checklist to make certain your actions are based on valid principles. You need these kinds of telescopic views before you move to ground level.

Dynamics of our personal change migration

James Canton, a future's expert, challenges us to constantly be in a mode of learning, collaborating, and discovering. We need to understand, manage, and leverage complexity, holding both disruptive change and amazing opportunities as the ultimate puzzle pieces. Canton uses the term "future-ready" as the capacity to leverage, monetize and adapt. Canton resonates with our philosophy and offers ongoing way finding for leaders.

KDi's leadership trends

Here are the attributes we have identified based on our work with governments and organizations in emerging countries on multiple continents. We provided this list in Chapter One, but now that you have a greater understanding of the Adaptive Path Framework and its role in sustainable change, we believe it is important for you to consider the list again from your more strategic perspective.

- Committing to alignment creates a common understanding of business objectives and strategy for change initiatives

- Focusing on communication so all expectations and concerns from key stakeholders are identified early in the process

- Modeling a culture of encouragement by building trust, support, and commitment for implementing change

- Acknowledging people's resistance by listening consciously to their fears, then address their concerns effectively. People often get onboard early and easily once their differences of opinion have been listened to and honored.

- Exploiting early success by involving people directly, whatever their job description, is an early indicator of success. Their enthusiasm spreads to others.

A client who was ready to lead from the front

When the Singapore Exchange (SGX) intended to outsource its data center and systems operations, the Information Technology Division of the firm realized the magnitude of change it had to deal with in a short span of time. Not only did the client have to deal with out-placing more than 50 staff, it also had to satisfy regulatory requirements for outsourcing and address a number of key stakeholders' concerns. We were engaged to facilitate a change communication plan to align all stakeholders' needs and interests.

Effected employees and key stakeholders were consulted in an open and supportive way. Addressing employees' fears and uncertainties head on not only reduced major impact to on-going operations but also developed trust and fostered commitment for adopting change. The migration to the outsourced data center operations was carried out through a technical roadmap as well as with an equally critical people-centric plan for communication.

With this client, the success of the transition to the new operational model eventually paved the way for more organizational transformation, strengthen its core business and leveraging external partners to support its non-core functions.

Leadership trends from the field

Mike Henry, who is with The Lead Change Group, a nonprofit community with 2,000 plus members, has found three changing trends in leadership development he deduced by watching the evolution of social media, the Internet, and the leaders themselves.

- Leadership development will become more personal.
- Leadership development will become more internal.
- Trial-and-error feedback loops will accelerate.

We also agree with the Lead Change Group that three other leadership development trends will continue. They include:

- Leadership development is learned, not taught.
- We still gain credibility the way we always have.
- We still grant respect the way we always have.

We have offered these guidelines from others as you begin your team's reflection on leading from the front.

Understanding basic human needs is essential

Will Schutz, a psychologist and author, identified three basic needs people have in interpersonal relations. These needs are also fundamentally important in people's reaction to change:

- Need for control.
- Need for inclusion.
- Need for openness.

At first, these basic needs might appear to be in conflict with each other. How is it possible to have control while being inclusive and open in all your communications? Let's shine a different kind of light on these needs. Control can be a positive need if it is based on collaboration. If control is ego-based, people recognize this immediately. The difference is in demanding lock-step formation versus leading from the front.

> **When we are under stress, there is a tendency**
> to revert unconsciously to our strongest unconscious behaviors,
> and it is easy to forget to use our consciously acquired leadership skills.

Daniel Goleman, who created the concept of human emotional intelligence and a popular test called the Emotional Competency Inventory, identifies adaptability on four different scales including:

- Openness to new ideas
- Adaption to situations
- Ability to handle unexpected demands
- Ability to adapt or change strategy

That covers the territory for leaders who are committed to their own excellence as leaders.

When Nancy was introduced years ago to Goleman's work, she took on the challenge of developing strengths in all four emotional competencies. For her, the weakest aspect was handling unexpected demands. And by the way, it is still her weakest adaptability skill, but she is now more consciously proactive when those unexpected demands are in her face.

Stress is an important reality to consider

Under prolonged stress, the part of our brain that solves problems with maximum efficiency goes on autopilot. There's a scientific reason why people in extended high-stress situations complain that they can't think straight.

Many people depend on you as a leader. You will be emotionally stronger and an infinitely more successful leader, if you take a few minutes each day to disconnect from the demands of the outside world. These down times need to be "intentional" and not periods for daydreaming about your next holiday. We recommend you start with a single concern or question and then make some notes about possible challenges and solutions.

Try some deep breathing exercises as a powerful way of transitioning from "busy brain" to "innovative brain." And remember not to engage in this activity if you are driving a car or on foot in a busy city!

Space that includes reflection is essential

As we have discovered, change does have a rhythm of its own. That's the reason the stages of Awareness, Acceptance, and Adoption are essential for your stakeholders to internalize change that sticks. And that same process applies to you! Does that come as a surprise? Or do you feel a bit of resistance when you realize you are thinking, "I am so overworked, and there are no minutes left for down time."

That's a predictable response for the workaholic mind-set we all share. But it's essential that we all learn to "override" that workaholic voice, at least for short periods. That's why we have suggested specific reflective questions at the end of each stage of the Adaptive Path. It is an issue of time and space for all of us as we take on new concepts, practice them in a safe environment, and then test them out.

But shouldn't it be easier than this? The answer is both yes and no. Yes, it would be more efficient if we could absorb change in an instant. Scientists tell us that our brains have learned as a survival skill to be skeptical of change. It's what allows humans to survive. While we aren't running from dinosaurs any longer, our nonverbal, emotional "ancient brain" doesn't recognize this. We override the resistance to change in ourselves by acknowledging the importance of paying attention to the needs for space and time in order to get comfortable with new ways of thinking and behaving. There is a reason innovative companies build in incubation time for managers and staff. They have determined that authentic sustainability requires time away from our task lists.

Embracing the Adaptive Path, with no final chapter

If you have spent your professional life working on a series of crisis interventions, you need to put that tactic in your rearview mirror.

You shouldn't simply get past the current crisis and then emotionally hide out, enjoying the respite until the next crisis appears.

You have now acquired some powerful strategies for leading sustainable change, but the questions must never go away. Quality questions take on issues as challenges to be solved. Here are some thought-provoking questions to begin your debriefing and reflective process:

- What have you and your team learned from your successes?

- More importantly, what have you learned from your failures, and how can they become successes when the next change initiative appears on the horizon? Don't be surprised if that change has already landed on your desk when you arrive at work tomorrow.

- How can failures be useful to your organization in the future?

- Where and how will you store these lessons learned so they are relevant and accessible the next time you need them?

Other questions will present themselves. You will discover new resources in yourself. Inspire them in others, and always be wise enough to get coaching for you and your team when you hit the wall or get lost in the maze, unable to find your cheese.

Our hope is that this book becomes a guide for professional and organizational change. Reading a book on change the first time can be an eye-opener. We have written this book in such a way that the second and successive reads should offer "aha" moments and then insights before they are actualized as strategies for leading sustainable change. We will all continue to learn, lead, learn some more, and, over time, lead even more effectively.

We believe you will benefit from our experience with clients in diverse parts of the globe. But instead of telling you how to do it, we model, demonstrate, and involve you so that, from the beginning of our engagement, individual and group learning becomes part of your organization's foundational strengths. This is our core value, and one we share with passion.

Reflection on Navigating Change

We strongly propose that these questions and your answers to them – or others you believe are relevant to your situation – become the foundation for reflecting regularly on what is happening in your world that validates the Change Facilitation Model.

Ask yourself:

- What still perplexes me about leading from the front?

- Where have I discovered examples that leading from the front is the best way to create awareness, cultivate acceptance, and facilitate adoption?

- In the context of winning hearts and minds, what strategies have I found that work best?

- As I review the important skills of my leadership, where am I comfortable with my progress, and where do I feel I need to do more conscious work? How do I feel I perform on:

  1. Openness to new ideas?
  2. Adaptation to situations?
  3. Handling unexpected demands?
  4. Adapting or changing strategy?

- What kind of verbal and nonverbal feedback do I get from others about my abilities to lead from the front?

- How is this feedback from others potentially helpful in my goal to be a leader who exceeds my own expectations by coaching leadership skills in others?

GLOSSARY

Acceptance
The process by which stakeholders embrace the change

Adaptive Path Framework
KDi framework activated as Awareness, Acceptance and Adoption

Adoption
The process by which employees at all levels acquire new skills specific to a change initiative and then use those skills to improve productivity

Appreciative Inquiry
Appreciative Inquiry is a shift from looking at problems and deficiencies and instead focusing on strengths and successes and is a tool for organizational change, designed to strengthen stakeholder relationships

Authentic Engagement
Giving your full attention to others, without judging so that outcomes are based on diverse perspectives

Awareness
The process where stakeholders are made aware of the impending change

Brand
A set of expectations, memories, stories and relationships that, taken together, account for a decision to purchase, or in the case of change initiatives, to become aware of, accept and adopt that change (definition attributed to Seth Godin and referenced in Chapter Six)

Change
Event or procedure that has deviated from the usual course of action

Change Agent
Someone who helps to champion the change

Change Cycle
Cycle of managing change through the process of Awareness, Acceptance and Adoption

Change Facilitation Model	A carefully orchestra four phase facilitation model based on Reframing, Planning, Implementing and Navigating The model supports and compliments our Adoptive Path Framework
Change Facilitation Team	A team of people from different parts of the organization who facilitate the Awareness, Acceptance and ultimately the Adoption necessary for the change initiative to have a positive impact
Change Support Network	Small group of carefully selected stakeholders who assist the change facilitation team in achieving Adoption, generally middle managers who have the trust of both their subordinates and their superiors and are the messengers that ensure people are at the heart of planning and implementing the change initiative
Clinic Sessions	An informal, collaborative meeting in which participants are walked through a new process, then participate in hands-on practice, guided by coaches
Change Communication Plan	Approach for communication with stakeholders on impending changes involving a variety of channels and media to heighten their awareness and reduce the uncertainties
Delay time	Learning that can be accessed by a person without having to be physically present to benefit and includes web sites, FAQs and videos
Executive Sponsor	Has ultimate accountability and authority for change initiative, coordinating with the team lead and approving milestones
Fact Sheet	Concise information that provide a quick overview of important specifications on a system or project
FAQs	An abbreviation for frequently asked questions

Focus Groups	A methodology intended to elicit reactions from participants on a specific topics in order to generate ideas and concepts that will help the organization better understand stakeholders' needs and concerns
High Touch/ Low Touch	High touch happens in real time, is face to face and interactive as opposed to low touch as passive experiences accessed by the individual in delay time
Knowledge Economy	Economy that relies primarily on the use of ideas rather than physical abilities and on the application of technology
OD	Abbreviation for Organizational Development as a deliberately planned effort to increase an organization's relevance and viability
Paradigm Shift	Change of one conceptual world view for another, more effective one
People Development	A term to describe the process of creating an organizational culture that supports people's ability to learn, relearn, refresh and reframe, based on the demands of change
Performance Learning Plan	Approach for transferring knowledge and skills to stakeholders to adopt new or enhanced organizational practices as a result of the change initiative
Performance Support	A system to support employee excellence, as informal as a supervisor coaching an employee, to sophisticated databases delivered to people's mobile devices. The goal is improved people performance, aligned with performance needs and instantly available at the moment of need
Real Time	Events and exchanges that are face-to-face, either in the physical or the digital realm

Resource Economy	Economy whose gross national product or gross domestic product to a large extent comes from natural resources
Return-on-Investment	A performance measure used to evaluate the efficiency of an investment or to compare the efficiency of a number of different investments
Road Show	A high energy, well executed event in which people learn a new process or acquire essential knowledge through interactive collaboration, resulting in empowerment to begin using a new skill on the job
Selective Perception	Mode of behavior in which a person interprets an event based on pre-conceived thinking
Stakeholders	All the groups necessary to the success of a change initiative
Stakeholder Engagement Plan	Approach for involving and interacting with stakeholders to build commitment and cultivate the acceptance of the change initiative
Steering Committee	A high level management team that reviews, provides strategic direction and gives final acceptance for a project deliveries
Stickiness	Ideas are understood, remembered, and have a lasting impact, a term from the book Made to Stick by Chip Heath and Dan Heath
Team Lead	In charge of all phases of project planning as well as implementation and reporting directly to the executive sponsor
Tipping Point	Defined as a "moment of critical mass, the threshold or the boiling point" and made popular by Malcolm Gladwell's book, The Tipping Point

END NOTES

Chapter One : Exploring Change as a Constant

Sarah Horowitz, Maya Enista, *Social Innovators Blog, Mobilizing for Change in the 21st Century*, http://www.socialinnovation.ash.harvard.edu/part-ii-mobilizing-for-change-in-the-21st-century.html (May, 2011).

Karl Weick, Kathleen M Sutcliffe, *Managing the Unexpected*, (San Francisco: Jossey-Bass, 2007), 2.

John P. Kotter, *Leading Change* (Boston: Harvard Business School Press, 1996).

Edward E. Lawler III, Christopher G. Worley, *Management Reset: Organizing for Sustainable Effectiveness*, (San Francisco: Jossey-Bass, 2011), 7 and 8.

Chapter Two : Overcoming Resistance to Change

Paul MacLean unlocked the mystery of human behavior with his triune brain theory. His theory is described in an article by Gustav Uhlich, *Our Triune Brain* in The Social Contract Press, Vol. 12 Number 3, http://www.thesocialcontract.com/artman2/publish/tsc1203/article_1071.shtml.

Thomas S. Kuhn, quoted in Eric Beinhocker's *The Origin of Wealth*, (Boston, Harvard Press, 2006), ix.

David Hu, in an interview with Richard Harris *Splish Splat? Why Raindrops Don't Kill Mosquitoes* was a story on National Public Radio which aired on June 5, 2012, http://www.npr.org/2012/06/05/154300189/splish-splat-why-raindrops-dont-kill-mosquitoes.

Chapter Three: Empowering Change

Art Markman, Psychology Today *Unpredictability Is in our Nature* http://www.psychologytoday.com/blog/ulterior-motives/200811/unpredictability-is-in-our-nature/comments (November 2008).

Twyla Tharp, *The Creative Habit: Learn It and Like It for Life*, (New York: Simon and Schuster, 2003.), 7.

Spencer Johnson, *Who Moved My Cheese*, (New York: G.P. Putnam and Sons, 1998), 63.

Steven Johnson, *Where Good Ideas Come From: The Natural History of Innovation* (New York: Riverside Books, 2010).

Chapter Four: Assessing Change Readiness

Edward De Bono, *Six Thinking Hats: An essential approach from the creator of lateral thinking* (New York: Little Brown & Company, 1986).

Chapter Six: Creating Awareness

Chip Heath, Dan Heath, *Made to Stick: Why Some Ideas Survive and Others Die*, (New York: Random House, 2007), 144 and 247.

Rosabeth Moss Kanter, *Five Tips for Leading Campaigns for Change*, http://blogs.hbr.org/kanter/2010/05/five-tips-for-leading-campaign.html, (May, 2010).

Seth Godin, *Define: Brand*, http://sethgodin.typepad.com/seths_blog/2009/12/define-brand.html (December 2009).

Hansa Marketing, *Delivering the Brand: Nine Principles of Change Management*, http://www.hansamarketing.com/blog/bid/238064/Delivering-the-Brand-Nine-Principles-of-Change-Management (March 2011).

Stephen Covey, from *The 8th Habit: From Effectiveness to Greatness* quoted in the book by Chip and Dan Heath's book, *Made to Stick*, 144,145.

Roger C. Schank, *Tell Me A Story: A New Look at Real and Artificial Memory* (New York: Charles Scribner's Sons, 1990).

Chapter Seven: Cultivating Acceptance

Olivier Serrat, *Appreciative Inquiry,* (Washington, DC: Asian Development Bank, 2010).

Chapter Eight: Facilitating Adoption

Laurie Bassi, In an online article titled *Measured Response*, David McCain referenced Dr. Bassi, who found correlations between an organization's commitment to training and its performance in the stock market, http://www.cfo.com/article.cfm/14577155 (June 2011).

Don Clark, *The Art and Science of Leadership,* http://www.nwlink.com/~donclark/leader/leader.html (October 2012).

Malcolm Knowles, *The Adult Learner: A Neglected Species* (Oxford England: Gulf Publishing, 1978).

Dr. Conrad Gottfredson and Bob Mosher, *Innovative Performance Support: Strategies and Practices for Learning in the Workflow* (New York: McGraw Hill, 2011), 37, 38.

Gabriel Radvansky, *Walking Through Doorways*, in an article by Susan Guibert published in the online Notre Dame News, November 16, 2011, http://news.nd.edu/news/27483-walking-through-doorways-causes-forgetting-new-research-shows/ .

Chapter Nine: Actualizing the Future

Jack Uldrich and **Simon Anderson**, *Foresight 2020: A Futurist Explores the Trends Transforming Tomorrow, http://www.amazon.com/Foresight-2020-Futurist-Transforming-ebook/dp/B008OXVAF4.*

Ernst and Young, *Business Redefined: A look at the Global Trends that Are Changing the World of Business*, http://www.ey.com/GL/en/Issues/Business-environment/Business-redefined---Understanding-the-forces-transforming-our-world.

Knoll Research, *Five Trends that Are Dramatically Changing Work and the Workplace*, a download of the full white paper is available on their website, http://www.knoll.com/knollnewsdetail/five-trends-that-are-dramatically-changing-work-and-the-workplace.

Woody Wade, articles on scenario planning from his website www.11changes.com http://www.11changes.com/scenario-planning/what-is-scenario-planning.html.

Pierre Wack, "The Gentle Art of Re-perceiving": : One Thing Or Two Learned While Developing Planning Scenarios for Royal Dutch/Shell *Harvard Business Review*, https://pure.strath.ac.uk/...wacks-the-gentle-art-of-reperceiving (September1985).

Chapter Ten: Leading from the Front

John Kotter, *The 8-Step Process for Leading Change*, http://www.kotterinternational.com/our-principles/changesteps/changesteps.

James Canton, www.FutureGuru.com.

Mike Henry, Lead Change Group, http://leadchangegroup.com/6-future-trends-of-leadership-development/ (October 2011).

Daniel Goleman, *Emotional Intelligence: Why It Can Matter More Than IQ* (New York: Bantam Books, 1996).

RESOURCES

Change Adoption Plan

Your goal in developing a Change Adoption Plan is to discern the impact of change on the stakeholders and to develop a coherent change facilitation strategy and action plans to facilitate the implementation of the organization change initiative.

The following table provides a structured way for you to organize your planning activities to analyze and assess the readiness for change and develop a highly effective first-cut strategy.

Activity	What to Analyze	Who are Involved	How can You be Sure
1. Change Analysis	It is important to identify the areas of the change in a large change initiative. Many areas from policy to operations, from job designs to technology systems could be part of the larger change initiative.	The sponsor can provide a strategic perspective of the initiative and clearly articulate the outcomes. The Project Implementation Team has the first-hand view of the initiative objective, scope and deliverables.	If the areas of change need to be clarified, validate with the Change Support Network and the Project Implementation Team.
2. Stakeholder Analysis	Any internal and external parties affected by the change or have an influence on the change. This could include management, employees, shareholders, partners and customers etc.	They can be affected in some small manner or in major way. Be as specific as you can when you determine which areas of change and how they affect the stakeholders.	Brainstorm with the help of the Change Support Network or consult with the representative of the stakeholder group to get more clarity.

Activity	What to Analyze	Who are Involved	How can You be Sure
3. Impact Analysis	Analyzing the impact of change on the stakeholders needs to be as granular as possible so that segments within the same group of the stakeholder can be further examined. For example, customers could be segmented into online and walk-in customers.	How each segment of the stakeholders are impacted should be given an impact rating of high, medium and low. High impact denotes change has an adverse effect on the segment if not managed. Low impact if the change has very minor effect on current way of doing things.	Asking the Change Support Network about the concerns or potential issues facing the stakeholder segment can provide a good sense of whether the impact is high, moderate or low.
4. Change Facilitation Strategy	Determining the readiness of the stakeholders is the most crucial part of this planning. Which stakeholder segments are most supportive of the change and which have signs of resistance. Articulate the strategy of securing support or addressing the concerns.	For each segment of the stakeholders, what actions can be brought to bear to mitigate the concerns. Identifying awareness, acceptance and adoption activities to meet the mitigation needs.	Validate the strategy with the Change Support Network and develop Change Communication Plan, Stakeholder Engagement Plan and Performance Learning Plan to implement the change facilitation strategy.

As described in Chapter 4, it is helpful to consider the three broad types of concerns: operational, emotive and assumptive. Identifying the source of a concern leads to greater understanding for mitigating those concerns.

The Readiness Assessment needs to be based on the types of concerns that stakeholders could be experiencing so your team knows how to target these areas. By categorizing the concerns, you are able to more effectively plan and enhance the approach as you move forward. In addition, you will need to consider the two dimensions of capability and preparedness. Readiness to adopt change has two dimensions. One is the level of capability for change, and the other is the level of preparedness for change.

Readiness Indicator	Interpretation	Potential Strategy
Confident	High Readiness – good capability and prepared to embrace the changes	Early adopter, empower to show the way. Involve in the pilot.
Competitive	Moderate Readiness – receptive to change but not too prepared for it	Need to focus on communicating the needs and performance learning.
Conservative	Moderate Readiness – good capability but has reservations about adopting the changes	Need to focus on communicating the benefits and engaging them to reduce doubts.
Contented	Low Readiness – not keen to make the change	Provide close support, communicate success and share best practices for adoption.

In general, the more ready the stakeholder is, the less resistance for adoption. You should revisit these readiness indicators throughout the project implementation so that you can evaluate your efforts at both the micro and macro levels.

Change Communication Plan

The Change Communication Plan provides a schedule of the communication activities that are to be carried out to heighten the awareness for the change initiative. These communication activities have to be derived from the Change Adoption Plan's Impact Analysis to address the concerns typically resulting from lack of visibility or information gaps in the implementation of the change initiative.

The objectives, target stakeholders, contents and timeline of these communication activities are essential elements to be flashed out in the plan. The following table provides a guide to develop such plan:

Activity	Objective and Stakeholder	Contents and Key Messages	Timeline
1. Branding of Initiative	A well-crafted brand gives identity, excitement and imagery to the initiative for all stakeholders.	Creating a logo and slogan for the initiative helps all stakeholders remember and grasp purpose of the initiative initiatively.	To be established and unveiled in the launch of the change initiative.
2. FAQs and Factsheet	All stakeholders new to the initiative like to know a few critical things about the initiative. The why, when, who and how are common questions to be answered clearly.	FAQs are essential in communicating common questions about the change initiative. Factsheet provides concise one-page summary of the purpose and scope of the initiative.	To be developed in the early stages of the initiative and updated along the way as more questions surfaced. FAQs can evolved to include adoption questions that can help clarify implementation details.
3. Announce-ments and Info Releases	Regular announcements tailored to specific stakeholders should be planned for to release key information about the initiative.	Highlights of the impending activities and involvement requirements for specific stakeholders are essential information to set the right expectations.	Three to four weeks before the impending activities set in. Long lead time may also be required for mobilizing certain groups of stakeholders.

Activity	Objective and Stakeholder	Contents and Key Messages	Timeline
4. Update Sessions	Regular update sessions to specific stakeholders to allow for clarification are critical to help them reduce uncertainties and dispel unwanted rumors or misconceptions.	Details of changes affecting the stakeholders and responses or involvements required to harness support from them.	Three to four weeks before the impending activities set in. Clarification should be acknowledged and followed-through with timeline.
5. Newsletter	Regular newsletter could be prepared to feature "human stories" to increase the level of interest to the initiative. Typically, done for internal stakeholders.	Highlights on what happened and positive reactions to the initiative. Voices of individual stakeholder featured to create strong impression of the reception.	From monthly to quarterly newsletter. Organizations with in-house newsletter could add special converge on the initiative without creating a separate newsletter.
6. Launch Event	Launch event to disseminate details and celebrate milestone achieved. Key representatives from various stakeholders are invited to the event. Token of appreciation provided.	Final details of the outcomes for the initiative are revealed. Recognition of specific stakeholders for support and contribution. Recognition for the Implementation Team	Ending stage of the initiative marking the transition to the operational stage.

Once these change communication activities are determined, a visual roadmap can also be prepared to provide an overview of the schedule in the form of timeline chart or calendar of events. The Change Communication Plan should be validated by the Change Support Network to ensure its relevance and timeliness for implementation.

Stakeholder Engagement Plan

The Stakeholder Engagement Plan provides a schedule of the engagement activities to be organized to interact with specific stakeholders to address concerns and challenges resulting from the change initiative. These concerns and challenges are operational in nature and would typically need participation, involvement with the specific stakeholders.

The objectives, target stakeholders, interaction format and timeline of these engagement activities are essential elements to be flashed out in the plan. The following table provides a guide to develop such plan:

Activity	Objective and Stakeholder	Interaction Mode	Timeline
1. Focus Groups	Gathering opinions and issues to understand concerns and explore potential solutions. Only very specific group of stakeholders are involved.	Small group of representatives are invited to provide responses to questions or clarifications on concerns.	Early stages in the initiative where concerns need to be understood or solution ideas are explored.
2. Games and Challenges	Exploring changing work patterns in a fun manner. Specific stakeholder groups impacted by the change in work.	An open invitation to participate in games or quizzes to bring more skeptics on board. Through fun and positive interactions, minds become open to change.	Early stages in the initiative where positive momentum is critical for the initiative that has been perceived as tough.
3. Community Meetings	Building trust through conscious listening and feedback for stakeholder groups that are highly critical of the initiative.	Visit the stakeholder groups to gain an understanding of the concerns or issues in in their "home grounds". Sincerity is key to getting support and eventual buy-in.	Early stages in the initiative where it has been established that certain grounds are "not sweet".

Activity	Objective and Stakeholder	Interaction Mode	Timeline
4. Feedback Channels	Harvesting reactions and responses to identify roadblocks to change. All stakeholders are invited.	Open to all stakeholders where feedback can be submitted through email or letter. Website's feedback page is also a good platform.	Throughout the whole initiative timeline. This is an ongoing process and assessment should be made to address all feedback in a timely manner.
5. Road Shows	Developing an interactive participation in new initiative to help. Specific group or entire stakeholders could be invited.	Stakeholders get to experience change in an interactive setting that galvanizes and improves readiness	Late stages in the initiative timeline when most details are worked out. Reactions to road shows should be closely monitored.

Engagement activities are time consuming and therefore, should be used to secure understanding on challenging issues and to create positive tone for the initiative. Similarly, the Stakeholder Engagement Plan should be validated by the Change Support Network to ensure its relevance and timeliness for implementation.

Performance Learning Plan

You are ultimately accountable for the success or failure of Adoption. Remember that while training managers develop the training programs, they are accountable to you for having those performance-based interventions be grounded in the strategic direction you, your team and the Change Support Network have committed to and acted on.

As team lead, your role is now to supervise the success of your initiative by having a committed, highly skill workforce that can meet the needs of change.

Using your increasing understanding of how to motivate others, you will be able to reassure the training professionals that you understand the basics of their job and appreciate what they do. We urge you to collaborate with them and make them feel valued, while you are absolutely clear that the ultimate decisions about how all six stages of the Performance Learning Plan are executed reside with you. Otherwise it will be business as usual.

ABSORBING	Focus on Performance Gaps	Effective Intervention	Performance Results
1. Experience	Identify performance gaps and preferred styles of learning	Face-to-face informal, interactive sessions using simulations and challenge games	Learners move past fear of the unknown to a belief that they can be successful
2. Train	Use information from stage one sessions for interactive new skill building	Workplace training with facilitator, reinforced by online sessions for individuals who need extra assistance	Learners demonstrate current level of competency as well as evidence of understanding new skill basics
3. Support	Continuous performance support available at the moment of need	Support online and through informal work related assistance with new skills	Learners are able to demonstrate independence, getting answers to their own questions

APPLYING	Focus on Becoming Competent	Effective Intervention	Performance Results
4. Coach	Coach observes and evaluates skill levels	Coach models intervening when needed in the learning process but also allows people to make mistakes, then learn from them *Access online support as needed*	Learners demonstrate new skill levels by performing tasks in which the coach points out strengths and gaps they still need to address.
5. Collaborate	Learners participate as equals with their coach in the final step to adoption	Learners demonstrate new skills and get feedback from each other and the coach *Access online support as needed*	Learners demonstrate abilities to take charge of their own learning Coach observes and evaluates progress
6. Facilitate	Learner becomes a workplace "mentor" for those employees just beginning the process of acquiring new skills	This new workplace role will give employees pride in helping others and will deepen their skill levels for their own job performance *Mentors point others to online support*	The results will be demonstrated in improved employees performance

And a final note:

This plan is, of necessity, a broad overview. It is radically different than the way traditionally training takes place. We know it works and are there to help you actualize a self-motivated workforce who takes pride in their performance and wants to help others do the same.

Made in the USA
Lexington, KY
07 January 2014